DAMN THE
TORPEDOES!

Captain Fraser, his wife Sheila, and son Powell stand in front of USS *Cape St. George* (CG 71) (Author's Collection)

DAMN THE TORPEDOES!

Applying the Navy's Leadership Principles to Business

CAPT. ALEC FRASER, USN (RET.)

Foreword by Adm. James Stavridis, USN (Rct.)

NAVAL INSTITUTE PRESS • ANNAPOLIS, MARYLAND

Naval Institute Press
291 Wood Road
Annapolis, MD 21402

Library of Congress Cataloging-in-Publication Data

Names: Fraser, Alec, 1949- author.
Title: Damn the torpedoes! : applying the Navy's leadership principles to
    business / USN (Ret.), Capt. Alec Fraser.
Description: Annapolis, Maryland : Naval Institute Press, [2016]
Identifiers: LCCN 2016003104 (print) | LCCN 2016011456 (ebook) | ISBN
    9781682470381 (paperback) | ISBN 9781682470398 (epub) | ISBN
9781682470398
    (pdf) | ISBN 9781682470398 (mobi)
Subjects: LCSH: Leadership. | United States. Navy. | BISAC: BUSINESS &
    ECONOMICS / Leadership.
Classification: LCC HD57.7 .F73 2016 (print) | LCC HD57.7 (ebook) |
DDC
    658.4/092—dc23
LC record available at http://lccn.loc.gov/2016003104

♾ Print editions meet the requirements of ANSI/NISO z39.48-1992
(Permanence of Paper).
Printed in the United States of America.

24 23 22 21 20 19 18 17 16   9 8 7 6 5 4 3 2 1
First printing

For Sheila and Powell

CONTENTS

List of Illustrations   ix

Foreword by Adm. James Stavridis, USN (Ret.)   xi

Introduction: General Quarters   1

1   A Day in the Life of a Navy Ship Captain   9

2   The Four Business Leadership Traits of Ship Captains   16

3   "No Excuse, Sir!": Accountable Leadership   24

4   "I'll Find Out, Sir!": Thinking and Learning Leadership   38

5   "Yes/No, Sir!": Ethical Leadership   53

6   "Aye, Aye, Sir!": Motivational Leadership   67

Conclusion: The Corner Office and the Captain's Chair   77

Acknowledgments   89

Notes   91

ILLUSTRATIONS

Captain Fraser and family	frontispiece
Aegis combat information center	1
USS *Enterprise*, USS *Porter*, USS *Nitze*, and USS *Vicksburg*	9
Induction Day at the U.S. Naval Academy	16
The damaged bow of USS *Wasp*	24
CNN Television Control Room	38
Costa Concordia	53
Japanese task force with USS *Kitkun Bay*	67
Captain's chair on USS *Midway*	77
The corner office	79

FOREWORD

A logical question to ask would be, "Does the world really need another book on leadership?" Hasn't everything already been said?

A lot certainly has been said about leadership, from the Bible to the Leadership Lessons of (fill in the blank), from Genghis Khan to Winston Churchill to Abraham Lincoln. But I would submit that this book of leadership lessons is authentic, timely, cleanly written, and deeply relevant to the business community today, something missing from so many books in this genre.

Let's start with authentic: Capt. Alec Fraser, USN (Ret.) is an American original. He has never pulled a punch nor has he puffed himself or anyone else up. He lives his life as the embodiment of the principles of leadership you will find in *Damn the Torpedoes!* From his beginnings at the U.S. Naval Academy through multiple command tours and especially his well-regarded leadership of Aegis cruiser USS *Cape St. George*, he has been a standout in inspiring his team, serving his sailors, and accomplishing the mission.

When I worked for then–Lt. Cdr. Alec Fraser on Aegis cruiser USS *Valley Forge* three decades ago, I knew I was part of a team. He perfectly balanced the need for mission success with caring for his entire wardroom and crew. Alec was at home with the extensive use of humor, high-energy creativity, and rock-solid integrity. He led from the front and made sure everyone in the four-hundred-person crew improved and developed even as we won awards and performed in real-world seagoing operations.

The book is also timely. As the business community seeks new leadership approaches, emerges from the 2008 market crash, and inculcates new standards of corporate behavior, the lessons of Navy life are plentiful and helpful. And Alec Fraser ought to know; he capped a superb career of command at sea in the Navy by becoming a president in Ted Turner's global enterprise. No one else can truly fuse the full experiences of both a successful Navy career and full business success as well as Captain Fraser.

Finally, it is well and truly written. It is worth noting that in a vast sea of turgid leadership jargon, *Damn the Torpedoes!* cuts across the rhetorical seas with clean, lean prose. Never verbose or wordy, this book can easily be digested and put to use in a day. It crackles with positive energy and leaves the reader smelling the tang of salt air, inspired to get under way toward new seas. As we say in the Navy, this is a book to which one can say, "godspeed and open water." It is destined to be a classic.

James Stavridis, PhD
Admiral, U.S. Navy (Ret.)
Supreme Allied Commander at NATO, 2009–13
Dean, the Fletcher School of Law and Diplomacy
Tufts University

General Quarters

Aegis combat information center on board the guided missile cruiser
USS *Vincennes* (CG 49). (U.S. Navy/Tim Masterson)

August 1864

"Damn the torpedoes! Full speed ahead!" yelled Adm. David Farragut.

Farragut was leading a line of Union warships into the well-defended entrance to Mobile Bay in August 1864. Confederate forts on each side of the entry channel were firing point-blank at his column, and a number of Confederate ships just inside the entry to the bay were firing in front of him. There were mines (torpedoes) anchored in the middle of the channel. It was a courageous attack against a well-defended entrance, and the Union ships were making progress.

Suddenly the lead ship struck a mine and blew up. Ships behind stopped, not sure of what to do while being engaged from three directions. That's when Admiral Farragut yelled his famous order that has been a battle cry for the United States Navy ever since: "Damn the torpedoes! Full speed ahead!"

The ships picked up speed, slipped past the forts, made it through the minefield, sank many of the Confederate ships in Mobile Bay, and thus closed the last main port of the Confederacy.

What led Admiral Farragut to give a command that could have resulted in disaster? It wasn't a snap decision. Without knowing it, he had been preparing for decades to issue that order by learning the four basic leadership traits of a navy ship captain.

This book is about those four leadership traits and how they can be applied by business leaders to make their careers and their companies successful. The four traits learned by Admiral Farragut were the same four I learned as captain of two U.S. Navy missile warships.

September 2015

The *New York Times* headlines on September 18th: "VW Is Said to Cheat on Diesel Emissions; U.S. to Order Big Recall." Over the coming weeks the evidence of a massive failure of leadership leads to the resignation of the chief executive officer, Martin Winterkorn. The extent of the cheating widens. The survival of Volkswagen is perhaps in question. Had the captain of VW learned and practiced the four leadership traits of ship captains, the scandal would have never happened, the future of VW would not be in doubt, and Winterkorn would still have his job.

November 1991

"This is not a drill! General quarters! General quarters! All hands, man your battle stations! Unidentified aircraft inbound!"

Our ship was in the northern Persian Gulf, near the Iraq-Iran border. I was in the after-gun mount when the general quarters alarm sounded. That's about as far as the captain of a U.S. Navy guided missile destroyer can get from his general quarters station in the ship's combat information center (CIC). Bad timing.

Sailors around me immediately started running to their assigned combat stations, taking preplanned and rehearsed actions: missile control radars were turned on, guns were manned, all four gas turbine engines were placed in operation, firefighting hoses were made ready, all doors and hatches were closed, and medical spaces were set for casualties.

While all of this was going on, I walked to my battle station. Walked. Not ran. It's important for the captain to show the crew a calm demeanor that makes them feel calm and confident, even if I am a little apprehensive. And there is no point in running. If action is needed in the next few seconds, there is little I can do. I fully trust the tactical action officer, a senior lieutenant to whom I had already given weapons firing authority to defend the ship if I was not in the CIC. There may be only a few seconds for him to take action. But I know this officer is ready.

I could walk because I was confident the crew was trained and ready to handle any challenge. They were confident in their skills. What I could do to handle an emergency had mostly already been done. So I walked—maybe a little faster than normal—to the CIC as sailors raced to their stations.

I felt confident the ship was ready in great measure because of my first sixty seconds at the Naval Academy.

I'll return to this emergency shortly.

Leadership at Sea and Business Leadership Ashore

This book is about the leadership traits of sea captains and how they can be used by leaders in any organization to make their careers and businesses successful.

What does a captain walking to his battle station have to do with business leadership? Some business leaders say that leading a business or a department is not like commanding a ship. They don't sound general quarters. They can't order people to act in the same way the military can order individuals into action. They don't make life-or-death decisions. Business is different.

But probably not as different as some think. Yes, business executives do not often make life-or-death decisions whereas ship captains do. Having to make such decisions creates a pressure that makes captains focus intently on their leadership style. The common traits of this leadership style have been refined over centuries, ever since the first ship went to sea without someone in charge . . . and did not come back.

My experience as a captain and a senior business executive has taught me that leadership ashore can very much be modeled after centuries of leadership at sea. Everyone does not need to face life-or-death decisions in order to learn. Constant awareness of the leadership traits of sea captains can make any manager more successful in a career and thus can make any business or organization successful.

Comedian Dick Gregory said, "When I was in the army, if I lost my rifle, I was charged eighty-three dollars. That's why captains go down with their ships."

I never had any intention of going down with the ship. Captains are not supposed to go down with their ship. We're the ones responsible for not letting the ship go down in the first place. How ships stay afloat and are successful in combat, and how their crews stay motivated, involve leadership traits every leader and manager can adopt.

The following chapters focus on the four key leadership traits of sea captains. Those traits can help propel careers, make businesses successful, make any organization more effective, help parents teach their children, help mentors mentor, and help any organization focus on its leadership style.

The leadership traits of ship captains can be used by any level of leader, manager, or anyone who aspires to be a leader or manager. They are designed to make readers think hard about what type of leader they want to be. Thinking about leadership is the main step to being a good leader.

As the following chapters will show, most of what I learned to be a successful ship captain I learned in the first sixty seconds of my plebe year at the U.S. Naval Academy in Annapolis. It took fifty pushups to learn these key lessons. This book will enable you to learn it without motivational pain.

Sixteen years after learning the key leadership lessons via pushups, I took command of a guided missile destroyer. As soon as I said, "I relieve you, sir" to the outgoing commanding officer, I felt the pressure of total accountability. I also felt ready because the lessons learned in that first minute at Annapolis had helped develop my leadership traits through the years. I didn't always do them right, and I could have done many much better, but I knew the traits of leadership backwards and forwards. I was confident. And when the alarm sounded on my ship in 1991, I could thus walk with confidence to my general quarters station.

This book offers a different perspective than most books on leadership. That's because I have had two careers: one as a ship captain and one as a business executive. I learned leadership at sea and what translates well to business and organizations ashore.

During my naval career I commanded two guided missile ships, one a destroyer (USS *O'Brien*) and the other a cruiser (USS *Cape St. George*). Both had terrific crews. The crew of the USS *Cape St. George* won the USS *Arizona* Memorial Award for being the most combat-ready surface ship in the entire Navy. How the crew achieved that award is a foundation of this book.

After my twenty-four-year career in the Navy, I had a second career in business as the president of Turner Properties, a division of Turner Broadcasting responsible for the building and operations of more than twenty-five Turner locations around the world. I was also an on-air military analyst for CNN and CNN International.

This book is based on my two careers and experiences. It is not a product of interviews or research. It is a product of experience afloat and ashore, and for that reason this book has a unique approach.

November 1991

Let's get back to the emergency of an unidentified aircraft approaching my ship at a high rate of speed.

I arrived in the CIC, the heart of the ship's operations and weapons control. It was a beehive of activity, with several dozen officers and crew members at their stations, controlling actions throughout the ship. Readiness reports were flowing in. Orders were going out.

The tactical action officer (TAO) was on the radio, issuing a warning to the unknown inbound aircraft: "Unknown aircraft bearing 030 degrees, range twenty-five miles. This is a U.S. Navy warship. Your intentions are unknown. Please identify yourself and alter course immediately." He then shifted circuits, and over our internal command net he briefed me on what was going on. I nodded.

A few seconds later he informed me all battle stations were manned and ready. The TAO then said something I had trained him and others to do: tell me what they intend to do and then do it. "Captain, the aircraft is still inbound. I intend to issue the next warning at fifteen miles. If he does not respond, I intend to follow our standard procedures with radars and weapons."

I nodded again. No need to say anything. He is listening and talking on an external radio circuit and two internal communication nets simultaneously.

The unknown aircraft is now fifteen miles from the ship.

"Unknown aircraft bearing 030 degrees, range fifteen miles, this is a U.S. Navy warship," the TAO says on the warning circuit. "You are standing into danger. Alter course immediately or we will take defense measures."

The aircraft continued coming.

The TAO then shifted to the internal command networks. "Missiles: illuminate aircraft with missile control radar. Guns: air action starboard. Hold fire. Prepare to place the close-in weapons system in automatic. Prepare to launch missile decoys."

The fire control system locks onto the aircraft with radar. Guns swing out on the side of the ship, ready to fire. The Gatling gun that fires a thousand rounds a minute at a missile or aircraft that gets too close is ready to fire. Decoys are made ready to fire to confuse any heat-seeking missile the unknown aircraft may fire.

We operate by negation in combat. If I had not agreed with anything the TAO was doing, I would have said so. I had nothing to say.

Suddenly the aircraft reverses course. Like in the movies, a warning buzzer sounds and a light flashes in the aircraft cockpit. The pilot knows we are serious about firing. As a line goes in the movie *Top Gun*, he is bugging out. He is obviously a military aircraft.

The TAO waits a few minutes until we have lost radar contact due to range, then he asks me for permission to secure from general quarters. "Permission granted," I reply. It's the first time I have spoken since the ship had been at general quarters. I then give a well done to the crew ship-wide.

The four leadership traits of sea captains I learned at the Naval Academy were in part responsible for how the crew responded to this emergency. I say "in part" because the crew at many levels also used the four traits. They, in the end, made the ship safe and successful. They showed that the four traits could be used at any managerial level. As we will see, the same traits can make a business safe and successful.

Why Read This Book?

How I was able to confidently walk to the CIC and then be able to say nothing during the emergency resulted from the four lessons on leadership I learned within the first sixty seconds of my training at the U.S. Naval Academy.

And there are five reasons why you should read this book:

1. It explains how centuries of leadership traits of ship captains can benefit careers, businesses, families, or any organization at any manager or supervisor level.
2. It's based on the author's experience at sea and in business. It focuses on what works at sea and ashore.
3. It's written to make you think about your leadership traits from a different viewpoint.
4. It's short and to the point.
5. It can help prevent a Volkswagen-type leadership failure.

So what are the leadership traits of sea captains that everyone can use in this modern, fast-paced, instant-decision, lack-of-time, and no-second-chance environment around us? What are the traits that allow us to walk confidently and say, "Damn the torpedoes! Full speed ahead!"? Read on.

A Day in the Life of a Navy Ship Captain

Aircraft carrier USS *Enterprise* (CVN 65), guided-missile destroyers USS *Porter* (DDG 78) and USS *Nitze* (DDG 94), and guided-missile cruiser USS *Vicksburg* (CG 69) transit through the Strait of Hormuz in 2012. (U.S. Navy/MC3 Scott Pittman)

July 1991

To understand the four major traits of leadership by ship captains, it's good to have some perspective on the job of a navy ship captain. It's a unique job, but there are still underlying leadership principles that are applicable to business and organizational leaders ashore.

One way to understand the captain's job is to look at a day in the life of a ship captain. In many ways the challenges, decisions, situations, and people are not that much different from what leaders ashore experience. I've chosen a day when my ship, the destroyer USS *O'Brien*, was approaching the Strait of Hormuz, the entry into the Persian Gulf.

The Strait of Hormuz contains two busy ship channels, one inbound and one outbound. While there is some order in the transit lanes, the approaches to the lanes are a free-for-all. At any given time, dozens of oil tankers approach the strait in both ways. Not far to the north is the coast of Iran, a nation not friendly to the United States. Iran has surface-to-surface missiles that could easily be fired from anywhere ashore. A targeted ship would have only a few seconds to respond. On the day in question, the weather is hazy with a temperature around 101 degrees Fahrenheit.

0530: Officer of the deck calls with the standard morning report:

"Good morning, Captain, this is the officer of the deck. The time is 0530. Sunrise will be at 0614. We are on course 350 at a speed of sixteen knots. The weather is hot and hazy with visibility about eight miles. The wind is from the south at eight knots. Gas turbine engines 1A and 2B are online. Damage control condition yoke is set. The ship's position is seventy-five miles south of the entry to the shipping lane that separates ships entering and leaving the Persian Gulf. There are six surface ships headed in that direction around us. My intention is to maintain course and speed for the next hour."

"Very well," I reply. "I'll be on the bridge in a few minutes."

I make a mental note that we are scheduled to launch a helicopter before passing through the straits at about noon and may have a problem doing so with the wind in the wrong direction. I know gas turbine engine 2A is not available due to preventive maintenance on its lube oil pump. It should be available by the time we reach the straits. I want to have all four engines available when we enter that restricted and dangerous passage. I've been awake for less than a minute and already I have to think ahead.

0545: The communications watch supervisor knocks at my door to deliver the overnight messages that have each been printed. It's done electronically today. There are sixty messages ranging from operational orders to weather reports to the shipping status of some critical spare parts needed for an electrical generator. The messages are also being read by the executive officer and the department heads. They will draft responses for me to approve should responses be needed. The day starts with an understanding of the big picture.

0635: I sit in my chair on the starboard bridge wing and review mentally for an hour our procedures on how we would respond to an Iranian small boat or missile attack in the next few hours . . . and next week's operations in the northern part of the gulf where an Iraqi attack is possible. I need to always be thinking ahead. Nice to sit outside before the sun makes the decks so hot you could cook eggs on them. We paint many horizontal surfaces on the ship white where we can to reflect heat.

0800: The messenger of the watch delivers the 0800 position report. While GPS is available, I still require the navigator or one of the officers to do a morning or evening star shoot. Fixing a ship's position by celestial navigation has been a part of sailing since ships first went out of sight of land. It's always nice to know how to get back to port without GPS.

0801: The executive officer and I have our daily meeting. He is the mayor of the ship in keeping the daily schedule moving along. We review the daily issues, and then we talk about transiting the straits. I want the two of us to be on the same page if something happens to me. He is second in command. Training him to be a captain someday is one of my most important jobs.

0830: We start a straits transit planning meeting in the wardroom. While plans have been made a long time ago, it's good to have the navigation team and bridge watch teams coordinated on the latest conditions. We talk through some potential problems that may arise. The tactical action officer (TAO) is there too. He will be the coordinator for defense in case we are attacked by missiles or small boats. Planning, training, and certification are the keys to operating safely at sea. The TAO has undergone a rigorous training program and has been personally certified by me to make tactical decisions should I or the executive officer not be immediately available.

0915: I visit sickbay. We have a terrific medical corpsman, but I always want to look at any ailing crew member. A sailor is running a fever, but he looks better than he did yesterday. If necessary, we can helicopter him ashore to Bahrain later today. It's important for the crew to know that the ship's leadership cares about them to the point that we will take extraordinary measures to get sick sailors ashore. We have an operating room if surgery is needed . . . such as in battle.

0925: I return to the bridge. The wild dash by ships in the area to get ahead of some slower ships before entering the channel has begun. There are strict rules of the road for who has the right of way and who does not, but not everyone follows them. One time years ago my ship passed near a small ship that did not have anyone visible on the bridge except a barking dog. Some guy then appeared, his eyes suddenly wide at looking up at a warship, and he grabbed the helm and turned away. Unbelievable things often happen when operating near the Persian Gulf.

1010: I review the daily intelligence report on Iranian and Iraqi operations and anticipated events. Nothing special is anticipated in the straits, but you can never know. It's amusing that a Persian carpet smuggler broke down in the gulf yesterday and was assisted by one of our ships until the Iranian Coast Guard arrived. The smuggler crew begged not to be turned over to the Iranians. The carpets were hidden under a layer of fish.

1015: We alter course for a few minutes to launch a helicopter. We were going to do this earlier except there were too many ships in the vicinity. We want the wind almost ahead when we launch. The helicopter will fly ahead and scout for armed small boats and anything else suspicious. Launching a helo off a rolling deck takes a lot of practice and a very detailed checklist, just like most ship operations. Checklists are the backbone of safe and consistently effective operations.

1030: As planned, we set battle stations on the ship for passage through the straits. There are Iranian antiship missiles on shore and on some of their ships. If they fire, we will only have a few seconds to respond with our surface-to-air missiles. I take my position in the CIC, where large electronic screens show all surface and air radar contacts. I can see the tactical picture better here. I command by delegation and negation. When seconds count, the tactical action officer issues orders, which I have authorized him to make. If I don't like what he is doing, I step in. The days of the captain standing with sword in hand on the quarterdeck as broadsides are fired are long gone. Today, delegation and command by negation are the hallmarks of effective combat operations.

1150: A centuries-old naval tradition continues. The messenger of the watch finds me in the CIC and says, "Captain, the officer of the deck sends his respects and reports the approaching hour of twelve o'clock. Request permission to strike eight bells on time, sir." I respond,

"Permission granted." Bells are rung every thirty minutes on the ship up to eight bells at noon, 4:00 p.m., and 8:00 p.m., and 8:00 a.m. We don't ring them overnight—no point in waking people up to tell them what time it is. 12:30 p.m. will be one bell, 1:00 p.m. two, and so on until eight bells at 4:00 p.m. Tradition makes the crew realize they are a part of centuries of sailors going to sea.

1215: The supply department cooks deliver sandwiches for lunch. Since the ship is at battle stations, eating on the mess decks is not possible. The cookie is really good.

1317: An outbound oil tanker suddenly alters course to pass directly in front of us. I am pleased with the way the officer of the deck (OOD) on the bridge responds without asking me what to do. He immediately orders the engines back full to stop the ship and sounds the danger signal on the ship's whistle. He calls the offending tanker on the bridge-to-bridge radio to tell him what we were doing . . . no need for any misunderstandings at a critical moment. The other ship changes back to her original course without answering the radio call. The seamanship on that ship is so bad I assume the chief chef must be driving it. I call the OOD on the speaker system to say well done. The entire bridge team, as I knew it would, hears my comments and hopefully that increases even more their confidence in making quick decisions. Training and certification pay off.

1500: We move out of the areas where an Iranian missile attack would be most likely. I order the ship to stand down from general quarters to the next lower level of battle readiness. Nothing has happened, but while we were at general quarters, the firefighting teams had conducted drills on extinguishing a fire in a main engine room and the gunnery teams had trained on safe handling of the ammunition. We will debrief the transit at the daily evening operations meeting.

1545: The XO and I review the weekly family gram we send to the families. We are going to be gone for more than six months, so communicating with families is one way to help them endure the long separation. If sailors know their families are happy, then they will feel better too. It's a part of keeping morale high.

1600: I conduct a maintenance inspection of the forward gun mount. I'm in coveralls with a flashlight to look into any dark areas. I want to see if any lube oil is leaking. There isn't. I pull one of the maintenance checks that was reported to have been done last week. The gunner who did it has to do it again while I watch. I want to know if he has been trained well and provided with the right tools to do his job.

1730: Another naval tradition: the offgoing junior officer of the deck knocks at my door and says, "Sir, the executive officer sends his respects and would like to invite the captain to dinner in the wardroom at 1730." The XO on a major naval ship is president of the mess. While the captain can eat anywhere, tradition is what makes the Navy special. I accept. I like to hear the latest jokes.

1830: I attend the evening brief attended by all the key officers and chief petty officers. We review everything that will happen overnight and the next day. Most of the discussion is on training shoots for our guns and firefighting drills on the helicopter flight deck. As always, training is going on twenty-four hours a day.

1930: I write a message to my boss, my commodore, discussing what we did today and what we plan to do tomorrow. The goal is to answer his questions before he asks them.

2000: The XO and I meet again. He reports the equipment status for the ship. We talk about the underway replenishment of fuel and food to take place tomorrow afternoon. The good news is that we will get some real milk; the powdered stuff has gotten old. The other good news is that the fleet is out of brussels sprouts. I hate them.

2036: Sunset. I always try to be on the bridge at sunrise and sunset. It's one of the reasons I like surface ships and not submarines. It's a great time to think. It's a great time to charge my batteries by reminding myself how much I enjoy being at sea.

2130: I wander around the ship. I take more time tonight because I was not able to do much of it during the day. The crew members who are not on watch or getting ready to go on watch at midnight are on the mess decks watching a movie. I chat with the engineer on watch in the after engine room. He has a six-month-old son at home who was born just three months before we left for our six-month deployment. His son and wife are doing fine.

2200: I sit on the bridge, watching the newest officer of the deck work the ship through a lot of oil tankers going the other way. He had been a junior officer of the deck for more than a year, so he has had some good experience. I had him go through a rigorous certification program before

I qualified him. If I am not on the bridge, he has the authority to take whatever action he thinks necessary to ensure the safety of the ship. For a twenty-six-year-old, that is a big responsibility. I am pleased with how he maneuvers. I don't have to say anything. Training and delegation again.

2330: I write to my wife and audio record another chapter from a book for my son. Since I am not home, my wife plays the recorded book chapter so he can hear me read him a story nightly. Being away from home for more than six months is hard.

2345: I call it a day, hoping for a few hours of sleep. Doesn't happen. I get a call from the OOD about every forty-five minutes about changing course to avoid other ships.

0530: A new day.

Questions for Discussion or Reflection

1. If you had to document a day like the one in this chapter, what would you list as routine events and what types of events would you list as nonroutine?
2. How many events in your day are affected by how well you have trained your team?
3. What is your personal training program? What is your business training plan?
4. Do you take time to just think?

The Four Business Leadership Traits of Ship Captains

Plebes carry their uniform items during Induction Day at the U.S. Naval Academy.
(U.S. Navy/MC2 Julia A. Casper)

June 16, 1968

At 8:35 a.m. I walked out the side door of the induction center at the U.S. Naval Academy, and in the next sixty seconds my life was changed forever. I didn't know it at the time, but I was being taught to learn the key leadership traits of being a sea captain and a business executive.

"Plebe!" yelled an upperclassman who appeared to be having a bad day. "Line up over here! Stand at attention! What's your laundry number?"

I was expecting something like "Welcome to the United States Navy!" But laundry number? How am I supposed to know my laundry number? I just got here. Nothing's dirty yet. Maybe I missed something in the mail.

"I don't know," I responded pleasantly, trying to improve the tone of the conversation. It didn't work. I noticed other plebes were having the same communications challenge.

He exploded with another yell, "Don't know? Don't know? Why don't you know?"

"No one told me my laundry number," I replied.

He looked me in the eyes and said, "That's no excuse! Drop for fifty pushups! When you get to forty-nine, stop halfway up!" I started my fifty and was now aware that most plebes around me were doing pushups too. The upperclassman was now asking the next guy coming out the door what his laundry number was.

At forty-nine, I stopped halfway up. I didn't know if he was counting, but I wasn't taking a chance. He came back over.

"Mister Fraser, there are only four responses here at the Naval Academy: Yes or no, sir! Aye, aye, sir! No excuse, sir! And I'll find out, sir! Got that?"

"Yes, sir!"

"What is your laundry number?"

I was a fast learner under pain. "I'll find out, sir!" I replied.

"Why don't you know your laundry number?"

"No excuse, sir!" I was learning the way to avoid pain.

"You have a welcome packet, don't you?" was his next question.

"Yes, sir!" I was beginning to think "welcome packet" may have been incorrectly named.

"Have you looked at it?"

"No, sir!"

"When I tell you to get up, look at it!"

"Aye, aye, sir!"

My laundry number was in the packet.

Little did I know those phrases would take up most of my verbal communications for the next year. Twenty-one years later I would use another traditional phrase, this one as a result of learning and using the four responses.

August 5, 1989

I was standing on a platform on the helicopter deck of the destroyer USS *O'Brien*, a Tomahawk missile–carrying destroyer. The outgoing captain was turning to me. A big moment was arriving.

"I am ready to be relieved," he said.

"I relieve you," I replied.

He turned to the admiral and saluted. "I have been relieved of command, sir."

I, too, saluted. "I have assumed command, sir," I reported.

With those two phrases I joined the centuries of ship captains who have gone to sea before me. The "I relieve you" phrase was possible because I learned the first four.

When I left the ship that evening, the ship's announcing system rang out with four bells and the petty officer of the watch announced, "*O'Brien*, departing." A pennant was hoisted at the mast to let other ships know the captain was not on board. I was not special. The announcement and bells had been made for every captain since the ship was commissioned. They would be made after I was relieved two years later.

Truth be known, the first time I heard the bells and announcement I almost looked around to see where the captain was before I remembered he was me. I had been looking around for twenty-one years. The habit was hard to kick.

All the bells, announcements, and other unique customs the Navy tradition gives a captain are there for one reason: to remind everyone of the captain's total accountability for the ship. When I left the ship, it was not "Fraser, departing." It was "*O'Brien*, departing." In a way, the captain is the ship.

A captain has a job like no other. I was totally—and I mean *totally*—accountable for everything that happened on the ship. Let it run aground even if I was not on the bridge, let its guns miss a target even if I was not firing them, or let a sailor injure himself somewhere on the ship even if I was nowhere close, I was held accountable.

Knowing I was accountable created a pressure to do the job correctly, the same pressure felt by sea captains for centuries. If I was not on the bridge when the ship grounded, why was the officer of the deck not better trained? If the guns were not hitting the target, when was the last time I had inspected them and not found a problem? If a sailor injured himself, had I made sure he was properly trained in what he was doing? And, oh, by the way, who certified the trainer?

I felt the tremendous pressure of the job.

But I also felt confident. Why was I confident? Because twenty-one years earlier I had learned the basics of being a captain in the four responses I learned after fifty, well, forty-nine and a half pushups. The responses were ingrained in me in the first minute and had molded my actions and thinking ever since, including my subsequent career at Turner Broadcasting. A captain has to think like a plebe, but from a larger sense of accountability. It's the same for any manager.

The Four Traits of Sea Captain Leadership

The four responses (I combine the "yes, sir/no, sir" response) the Naval Academy teaches are not something that just happens to fit the training of midshipmen. Behind each lies an attitude necessary to command a ship. My experience has shown those attitudes are necessary for any manager to advance a career quickly, for a business to be competitive, for an organization to be effective, and for a parent to lead a family.

Let's look at the four responses in a general manner and how they relate to leadership. The following chapters will cover each in detail. Four is all there are. After forty-nine and a half pushups, four is all you want.

Leadership Trait 1: "No Excuse, Sir!"—Accountability

In 1954 the destroyer USS *Hobson* was cut in half by the aircraft carrier USS *Wasp*. The ship sank, and most of the crew, including the captain, drowned. Though the captain was not aware of the impending collision until it was too late, he was still held accountable for the loss of his ship by a naval court of inquiry. The opportunities for collisions in fast-paced operations are many. Why there are not more collisions can be attributed to the acceptance of total accountability forced by the understanding that a captain has no excuse for anything that does not go right.

In my first seconds at Annapolis I learned quickly to assume total accountability. Initially, it was only knowing my laundry number. As the years passed and my career progressed, I never forgot there were no excuses if I did not achieve my goal of becoming a ship captain, no excuses for not performing an assigned mission, and no excuses for not keeping my crew safe. I could not blame my boss, my education, my training, my circumstances, the sailors in my department, the enemy . . . whoever or whatever. I could make no excuses if my career was not successful. The same was true at Turner Broadcasting. Shooting missiles was similar to shooting electrons to a cable satellite. It was up to me to make my career in a broadcasting company successful.

Years later, it was the accountability pressure of command to make sure everything possible was being done to ensure that a mission was completed successfully and safely. There were no excuses if the mission was not done safely. If a captain thinks someone else can be blamed if something goes wrong, the captain loses the pressure of accountability. When the captain loses that sense of accountability, things go wrong. People get hurt. Ships sink. In an organization on shore, a lack of a sense of accountability leads to budgets not being met, sales not being competitive, quality control deficiencies, labor issues, and business or organizational failure.

Ashore, the pressure of total accountability can provide the motivation for leaders to understand they are responsible for more than just their job description. All leaders or managers are responsible for the success of their businesses, particularly the decisions of the boss. "Not my department" should be stricken from our vocabulary.

No excuse means accepting total accountability. Chapter 3 describes how organization leaders can adopt this attitude.

Leadership Trait 2: "I'll Find Out, Sir!"—Learning and Thinking Ahead

Iraqi aircraft were armed with French Exocet air-to-surface missiles that home in on a ship by using the missile's own radar. How to best engage an incoming missile was something the crew had to learn. "Nobody told me that" would be a poor reason for a ship to get hit. So I needed to know and to train my crew to know too. They were, of course, highly motivated to know. We found out how best to engage Exocets. Nobody had to tell us to learn.

Plebes at Annapolis are told the story of an aide to Theodore Roosevelt. The aide was called to Roosevelt's office one day and told to deliver a letter to Garcia. Roosevelt did not say who Garcia was or where he was. The aide did not ask. He found out the answers to the questions on his own and delivered the letter to the leader of the Spanish government in Cuba. Plebes at Annapolis are taught the "letter to Garcia" lesson.

From the first sixty seconds of my naval career through my retirement from the Navy, the "I'll find out" attitude was a driving force in learning how to confidently command a ship. It took twenty-one years of learning about weapons, engineering, fleet operations, and supply support to be able to sleep better at night at sea. It was my job to learn and not expect to be taught.

The need to find out did not stop with assuming command. If anything, the pressure to learn what I did not know increased. There was no excuse for not knowing. I had to think ahead intensely to determine what I needed to learn.

Ashore, creating personal and organizational attitudes of "I'll find out" can be effective in making any business or organization competitive in the marketplace. For example, knowing the product, the customer, changing market dynamics, employee training, costs, etc., should be continuous learning efforts by leaders. The "nobody told me that" response should be stricken from our vocabulary for career and business success.

Chapter 4 shows how personal learning and organizational training can create a "find out" mentality.

Leadership Trait 3: "Yes, Sir!/No, Sir!"—Ethics

"Did you polish your belt buckle?" the upperclassman asked me one day at Annapolis. If I said "No, sir," I would get demerits that would result in walking a few formerly free hours with a rifle. If I said "Yes, sir" and had shined it, I obviously had not done a very good job and would receive some demerits anyway. If I said "Yes, sir" and had not shined the buckle, the lie would result in an honor offense for which I could be dismissed from the academy. A naval career could be ended by not telling the truth about shining a belt buckle.

"Dismissed for a belt buckle?" people ask when I tell this story.

It's not about the belt buckle. It's about always telling the truth. It's about right and wrong. It's about ethics. It's about building trust with a crew.

At sea, a crew depends on each other to keep their ship afloat. On any given day the failure of some critical piece of equipment could endanger lives. To prevent failures, the Navy has detailed maintenance plans and procedures. If maintenance is not done when needed or not done correctly, the ship could fail during a mission and lives could be lost.

That's why when my ship went to general quarters for the inbound unknown aircraft in 1991, I was inspecting the maintenance and training of the ship's electricians. I was confirming that maintenance had been conducted correctly on an electrical system as it had been reported to me. For a crew member to say he had done the maintenance check and not done it is a violation of trust. Lives depended on the working of the electrical generator. The crew has to trust each other to do their jobs and be truthful about what they do.

Ashore, trust is key to an organization's success. Many people have lost trust in large companies or government. They have a right to lose that trust. Interestingly, Airbnb is an example of how trust in peer-to-peer organizations is growing. Trust can be developed.

Companies and organizations can create trust by the leaders always saying yes or no honestly. Ethics still count. We all know that. Why don't we all do it? Chapter 5 shows how important a leader's personal code of ethics is to the success of an organization.

Leadership Trait 4: "Aye, Aye, Sir!"—Motivation

In 1898, at the start of the Spanish-American War, Adm. George Dewey and the Pacific Squadron steamed into Manila Bay in the Philippines and attacked the anchored Spanish fleet. As the American ships closed the range, Dewey turned to the flagship gunnery officer and said the famous words that all plebes at Annapolis must memorize: "You may fire when you are ready, Gridley."

"Aye, aye, sir!" was the response. Not "okay." Not a simple "Yes, sir."

Naval language is a language of its own. Terms like "deck" for a floor, "bulkhead" for a wall, "starboard" for right, or "scuttlebutt" for a water dispenser are all examples. So is "aye, aye, sir!"

A sailor responds with "aye, aye, sir" when he or she agrees to perform something that a more senior officer or petty officer (that's another term for an enlisted leader, as in chief petty officer) asks or orders. It's an interesting term because it shows more enthusiasm for performing a task than "I'll do it" or "okay." The term connotes a motivation to do the assignment quickly, correctly, and with a positive attitude. It's hard to say "aye, aye, sir!" and not show enthusiasm.

"Aye, aye, sir" shows motivation because the response is rooted in a sailor's belief that what he or she is doing is important. It's not just the task being assigned; it's the reason the task is being assigned that is motivating.

When sailors take the oath of enlistment or officers take the oath of a commission, the oath in part says that they will "support and defend the Constitution of the United States." That may sound outdated to many people, but it doesn't to members of the military. It is the reason they do what they do. The reason they put their lives at risk.

In businesses, motivation can obviously not be created by having the employees take an oath to defend the Constitution. But it can be created once leaders know why people do their jobs in their organization. Leaders know what their employees do and how they do it, but how much do they know about why they do it? The "aye, aye" enthusiasm can be created ashore as well as at sea. Chapter 6 shows how employees can be motivated like sailors at sea.

In summary, what I learned in the first sixty seconds of my naval career was the foundation to being a ship captain and business executive. The foundation was in the four responses I learned: I'll find out, no excuse, yes or no, and aye, aye. Years later I would be using and instilling the attitudes inherent in those phrases to command ships at sea. They would keep the ship afloat and the crew safe.

In my career at Turner Broadcasting, most definitely not a military-style organization, I learned that the same foundations can apply without the pressure of having to make life-or-death decisions. The following chapters show how.

Questions for Discussion or Reflection

1. What are the key traits of your leadership style?
2. Can you put your leadership philosophy in writing? Try it.
3. Who taught you about leadership and what did you best learn?
4. Are you teaching others your leadership philosophy?

3

"No Excuse, Sir!"
Accountable Leadership

The damaged bow of USS *Wasp* (CV 18) after colliding with and sinking
USS *Hobson* (DD 464). (U.S. Naval Institute Photo Archive)

May 1915

"Torpedo coming!" yelled the starboard lookout of the RMS *Lusitania*.

"Hard to starboard!" yelled Captain Turner to the helmsman. But it was too late to turn to avoid the torpedo.

Seconds later the torpedo fired by a German U-boat exploded on the starboard side, sending a geyser of water, bits of coal, wood pieces, and metal into the air. A second explosion somewhere forward inside the ship quickly followed. The bow started to go down and a starboard list developed quickly.

"Full astern!" ordered Captain Turner. But the engines did not respond. He ordered the helmsman to steer toward the Irish coast clearly visible to the north. But the helm did not respond. At eighteen knots, water was being forced into the ship.

"Lifeboats to the rails," ordered Captain Turner. The ship was moving too fast to order abandon ship. The list to starboard increased as the bow sunk lower and lower. Power and lighting was lost throughout the ship. Passengers in elevators were trapped.

Panic quickly developed in the nearly two thousand passengers and crew. There had been no lifeboat drills; passengers were not assigned to specific lifeboats; there had been no instruction on how to correctly don a life jacket.

With the bow now going under water, Captain Turner gave the order to abandon ship even though the ship was still moving fast. There was chaos on the lifeboat decks. Many of the crew had not participated in a lifeboat drill. Almost none had practiced lowering a fully loaded lifeboat, a procedure that requires close coordination between the crew members.

Several boats in the process of being lowered tipped over, spilling the passengers on board and then dropping on top of them. One boat made it to the water intact but quickly sank because a crew member forget to put the plug in a drain hole in the bottom of the boat.

Of the twenty-two standard wooden lifeboats, only seven were launched successfully. As the twenty-two lifeboats could only hold about half of the passengers, the ship was equipped with canvas-sided "collapsible" lifeboats. Almost none of these were launched because there had been little crew training on how to launch them. Many could not be launched because they were glued to the deck from frequent painting or were secured by rusted bolts that could not be loosened. Captain Turner had decided not to loosen them in a war zone because they might slide across the deck.[1]

Eighteen minutes after the torpedo hit the *Lusitania*, the largest and fastest passenger liner of its time sank. Of the nearly two thousand passengers and crew, only 764 survived. More should have.

Two formal inquiries were conducted to determine accountability for the disaster. Why did the ship steam in known U-boat-infested waters? Why didn't the British navy provide an escort? Why did the ship sink so quickly? Why were so many passengers and crew killed? Should the captain be held accountable?

Both inquiries found only the German navy responsible. Captain Turner was not held accountable, even though proper crew and passenger training could have saved hundreds of lives.

Captain Turner did not hold himself accountable either. In an interview with the *New York Times*, he said, "I am satisfied that every precaution was taken and that nothing was left undone that might have helped save human lives that day."[2]

The absolution of Captain Turner by civilian-based inquiries was wrong. He was at fault for not training his crew correctly. Had the British or American navies conducted the investigation, he would have been held accountable.

The collision between the USS *Wasp* (CV 18) and USS *Hobson* (DD 464) and the subsequent assignment of accountability is an example of what should have happened to Captain Turner for the loss of life on the *Lusitania*.

April 1952

On the night of April 26, 1952, the destroyer USS *Hobson* and the carrier USS *Wasp* were in formation while the carrier was conducting flight operations. At one point, when the carrier needed to swing into the wind to recover aircraft, the *Wasp* put out a signal indicating the turn. The *Hobson* tried to cut in front of the carrier to change station, but it collided with the *Wasp* and was cut in two, and 176 sailors, including the captain, were lost.

At a subsequent Board of Inquiry, the captain, even though he went down with the ship, was found responsible for the collision and sinking. Unlike Captain Turner on the *Lusitania*, the commanding officer of the *Hobson* was held accountable.

A No-Fault Leadership Culture

The *Wall Street Journal* wrote an editorial titled "Hobson's Choice" about the collision. It discussed the difficulty we all have of holding good people accountable who erred in judgment under immense pressure. There is a feeling, it stated, that being human absolves people of accountability; at sea, however, it is different.

Responsibility and authority are given only with accountability: "This accountability is not for the intentions but for the deed. The captain of a ship, like the captain of a state, is given honor and privileges and trust beyond other men. But let him set the wrong course, let him touch ground, let him bring disaster to his ship or to his men, and he must answer for what he has done. He cannot escape."

The editorial concludes with a statement that is as valid today as it was back then: "It is cruel this accountability of good and well-intentioned men. But the choice is that or an end to responsibility and finally, as the cruel sea has taught, an end to the confidence and trust in the men who lead, for men will not long trust leaders who feel themselves beyond accountability for what they do.

"And when men lose confidence and trust in those who lead, order disintegrates into chaos and purposeful ships into floating derelicts."[3]

Businesses and politicians can become derelicts too. The graveyard of corporations is littered with those companies whose leaders did not have a core value of accountability. "Mistakes were made" is a common corporate admission of failure without holding anyone accountable. Politicians often give a common response to a failure of judgment: "I made a mistake. Let's put that in the past and move on." In other words, "do not hold me accountable." And no one does.

The whole concept of a corporation is designed to prevent individual accountability. In September 2015 General Motors was fined $900 million for not correcting a known flaw in an ignition switch. To date no criminal charges against any executive have been filed even though the prosecutor showed that some executives made fraudulent statements. The mother of a child killed by a car that crashed due to the faulty switch said in a statement, "While nothing can bring my daughter back, we need a system where auto executives are accountable to the public and not just corporate profits."[4]

There may be hope that executives who deliberately take actions that are known to possibly injure people may be held more accountable, at least in the food industry. In October 2015, Stewart Parnell, the owner of a company that made peanut butter that was linked to a deadly salmonella outbreak, was convicted and sentenced to spend twenty-eight years in prison. One e-mail he sent about a batch whose testing had been delayed read, "Just ship it. I can't afford to [lose] another customer."[5]

The culture of no-fault leadership by some business and government leaders may not have changed much since 1915 or 1952 or 2015, but operating in that environment can be countered by a leader who adopts a "no excuse" attitude.

The Pressure of "No Excuse"

The Navy has the mind-set of "no excuse" for any decision that adversely affects the safety of a crew. That's why the captain of the *Hobson* was found guilty of negligence. It does not make any difference if he was not personally involved. If the captain did not trust the officer of the deck, he should not have qualified him for the job. It's the captain's job to train and certify the officer who is responsible for ship operations when the captain is not on the bridge. So the captain is still responsible.

The intense accountability pressure on ship captains to do everything possible to make sure mistakes are not made is the reason so few mistakes are made. This is the key to effective leadership by anyone at any level in any organization.

There are hundreds of things that could go wrong on a ship every day that could sink it. There were days at sea when some things did not go right. I'd remind the crew on those days that we were afloat because thousands of things were done right.

That ships seldom sink is for the most part due to the fact that captains enthusiastically embrace the personal accountability they assume with command. They accept it; it affects every waking moment; it disciplines thinking; it creates honesty. Business and organization leaders can learn the same attitude of total accountability without having to make life-or-death decisions.

The pressure to be ready to make decisions creates a captain's mental attitude of total accountability. Effective business leaders need to have the same pressure created by a sense of total accountability that ship captains have had for centuries. The pressure of that mental attitude avoids collisions and keeps ships afloat. It can make a business more successful too.

Why a Mental Attitude of "No Excuse" Accountability Is Vital

"You the man!" or "You the woman!" is never a yell from the crew when the captain approaches. Can you imagine a century or so ago if a crew member had yelled that? He'd probably have gotten a dozen lashes or even been hanged. It is a slogan, however, that applies to a ship captain more than anyone else. The captain is "the man" because he or she is the one who is totally accountable. A ship does not work safely or effectively any other way.

Accepting total accountability creates a state of mind of being personally ready. With that state of mind, a captain works hard at thinking ahead, thinking about what can go wrong and then planning and training himself or herself and the crew to meet the anticipated challenges. With the lives of the crew at stake, immense pressure is on a captain to be ready to make quick, correct decisions. Though not under the same pressure, this same mental attitude of accountability can be adopted by business managers too. There are several reasons why this attitude is vital to effective leadership.

Accountability Pressures Us to Act

"Would someone please make a decision?" That's not a complaint at sea. A captain is obviously motivated to decide to fire missiles at an attacking enemy aircraft, motivated to decide on a safe course between rocky islands, or motivated to decide what port the sailors would most like to visit in the Mediterranean. (Hint: It has little to do with museums.)

In business, we may not have enemy missiles headed at us to stir our motivation, but we need to have something similar to pressure us to make decisions. That something is the pressure for a successful career and a meaningful life, and to help our employees have a successful career and meaningful life too.

If we want to be a senior vice president or a managing director, we need to assume total accountability for achieving that goal. No excuses. With that as our goal, we should be motivated to make our department and business successful. To do that, we need dedicated and trained employees who also want a successful career.

But we already know all that. What does a captain do differently than most of us? A captain prepares for decisions based on the intense pressure that motivates him or her to be ready to make decisions. Like the Boy Scout motto, "Be prepared," good managers develop that sense of pressure. Those who are successful are the ones who become senior executives and managing directors.

Accountability Disciplines Us to Think and Plan

"Why didn't I see that coming?" Not a good thing for a captain to say when an enemy torpedo hits the ship. But we all say that when we're surprised. Well, why didn't we see it? If whatever *that* may be is a thing for which we are responsible, did we try to think about it in advance and plan a response?

If we wander around a Navy ship, we find there is only one chair on the bridge. There is not just one chair because an interior decorator thought it looked good. It's there because a captain must be on the bridge for hours, and it's also a place for the captain to sit and think. I would sit in my chair thinking, watching, listening to what was going on in the ship and the miles of sea around the ship. Accountability made me think in the long and short term. I needed to be proactive, not reactive, in my decision making.

If we feel accountable, we know we need to think about situations we may need to face in our career and business and be ready to respond.

Accountability Increases Success: For the Business and for Our Careers

"Not my job." Hear that from a crew member or employee, and we can be pretty well assured that person will never go far in a management position. Captains can never say that. Successful managers and leaders should never say or think it either.

Good officers get noticed because they look beyond their regular job descriptions. Interesting, too, that these officers, without being asked, helped other officers when the going got tough for one of them. Some of those officers are now commanding officers themselves.

The pressure of accountability for the success of our careers and businesses should force us to look outside our job description to ensure the success of other departments. A front desk manager of a hotel should feel responsible for helping the engineering department do its assignments. That's good for the hotel. It also means fewer complaints. An accountant can provide operational recommendations to the manager of a production line. The pressure of accountability should make us all try to help others in our company, even if they are peers in competition with us for a promotion.

Accountability Forces Us to Have a Personal Code of Ethics

"What happens in Vegas stays in Vegas." That may be the best example of the worst ethics. What we do in Las Vegas is a reflection of who we are. If we feel accountable to ourselves, our families, our employees, and our community, we have a defined idea of right and wrong that does not change at the gangway or office door.

A sea anchor is a big mass of anything—mattresses, boards, sheets, etc.—that can be tied together and thrown overboard with a line attached to a ship. Since a ship that is not under power is mostly affected by the wind, putting a sea anchor over in an emergency when the water is too deep for the normal anchor helps keep the ship pointed into the wind and, thus, the waves as well. The mass does not stay in one place, but it is not affected by the wind as much as the ship is. Thus a ship can stay pointed in a safe direction during a loss of power during a storm. A sea anchor can keep a ship from capsizing.

A Navy ship captain cannot earn the respect and trust of the crew unless that captain is fair, consistent, and honest. To do that the captain must have a code of ethics, which, like a sea anchor, keeps him or her pointed in the right direction, because the mass is the captain's perception of right and wrong. Accountability forces us to determine what is right and wrong, to make decisions consistently, and to always tell the truth. From that a captain earns respect. The same is true of business leaders. There is no difference ashore in gaining respect for ourselves and gaining the respect of others.

Eight Steps for Creating "No Excuse" Leadership Accountability

"Right full rudder, all engines back emergency, sound the collision alarm, prepare to abandon ship, send an SOS!" I yelled. The ship was approaching a shallow reef at flank speed.

Then I woke up. Another nightmare that the pressure of accountability seemed to cause. Captains have a name for that sleep-ending dream: the rocks and shoals nightmare. Years later, ashore, I still have them.

Thank goodness managers don't have rocks and shoals nightmares, but we still need to create something with the same intense pressure of accountability that hopefully stops short of nightmares. Without fear of getting seasick, listed below are some steps managers can take that can help to develop a vital leadership mental attitude of total accountability.

Assume Total Accountability for Our Careers

"Captain, I screwed up," I said as a new ensign on the bridge of my first ship assignment. I had taken the wrong station in a fleet maneuvering exercise with some other ships.

The commodore of the squadron broadcast on the common radio circuit that all the ships were monitoring, "That is the worst naval maneuver I have ever seen!" I had made my ship look bad, although I couldn't figure out why the commodore had seen so few maneuvers that he thought this was the worst. I already had seen, and done myself, a lot worse. I thought that since my naval career and any promotion was over, I might as well admit it before getting chewed out by the captain.

Fortunately, I didn't have to update my résumé, but the incident did focus me on ship handling, a vital requirement for my career goal of being a ship captain. I worked to get better and eventually won the squadron ship-handling award from the same commodore who apparently had (probably deliberately) a short memory. Even today I vividly remember the exercise because it made me focus more on my career plans and how I was working to achieve them. I learned some lessons along the way.

Forget thinking about the common excuses for not getting promoted: the boss' unfairness, poor education, poor training, incompetent employees, poor business environment, lack of leadership, bad timing, or "I never had a chance." With any of those excuses, we most certainly didn't have a chance.

We need to assume career accountability by realizing that excuses will not get us promoted. We get promoted by constantly training ourselves to better do our current jobs, constantly training ourselves to do our boss' job, creating a plan to get us where we want to be in five or ten years, and then following the plan. It's that simple. But if there is no self-imposed sense of accountability, there is no pressure to create a plan, and so a good plan is never created. We become reactive instead of proactive.

Learn to Do Your Boss' Job

"I relieve you, sir," I said as I formally took command from the previous commanding officer of the USS *O'Brien*. "I stand relieved," he replied.

From the beginning of my naval career I was a line officer, meaning I was eligible for command at sea even as an ensign. If in battle it ever came down to the fact that I was the senior officer still standing, I would become the captain. Probably much to the relief of some crews, that never happened.

Being eligible did not mean I would be guaranteed to get the captain's job under normal circumstances. I had to learn it first. The best career-enhancing move for all of us is to learn how to do our boss' job as well as we perform our own job. That takes a conscious effort, hopefully as a part of our career plan.

Be Accountable for Your Employees' Success and Morale

Everyone knows grog is a sailor's drink—a mixture of water and rum—given years ago to crews at sea twice a day. It was the key to morale. And it makes many of us groggy.

Grog was developed by English admiral Edward "Old Grogram" Vernon. Grogram was the material used for the admiral's waterproof coat, so the sailors named the new drink grog in honor of him. And by the way, Mount Vernon, the home of George Washington on the Potomac River, was named after Admiral Vernon, but probably not because of grog. And further, officers did not have to mix water with the rum, hence their serving was called "neaters."

Providing grog to crews should remind us of our accountability to the crew and our employees not only for their morale but for their career success as well. Morale is something beyond just grog and company picnics. How it's done is unique to each company, but it starts with understanding what motivates the group. A later chapter discusses this topic in detail.

Be Prepared to Say "No Excuse"

"I will never trust anyone anymore because this was a very deadly mistake," said Francesco Schettino, the captain of the *Costa Concordia*, after running his ship aground. Thirty-two people died in the accident. Schettino blamed his officers for the grounding.

It's obvious to me why "Captain Coward," as he has become known, abandoned his ship before all the crew and passengers were evacuated: he had no sense of accountability. His blaming of his officers for the grounding shows he was not ready to say there was no excuse for his own actions.[6]

Not being able to immediately say "no excuse" means he did not have a no excuse attitude to leadership. Not having that attitude means he did not feel the pressure to make sure everything possible, including the training and supervision of his officers, was done to ensure the safety of his ship. If we are not able to default immediately to saying "no excuse" when something happens, we are not good leaders.

Take Time to Think

"Time, tide, and formation wait for no one!" yells a plebe on every floor at the Naval Academy exactly one minute before everyone is to be formed into ranks outside. That plebe then has to get to the formation that may be exactly sixty seconds away at a fast run. Being late means demerits, which means walking with a rifle for a few hours on the weekend, which perhaps means calling his girlfriend and telling her he can't make it that weekend.

So an awareness of time is a major naval trait that is painfully instilled in midshipmen from the first day. That same awareness disciplines a captain to understand that he or she must take time to think about what likely will happen in the future and how best to respond to those challenges. Accountability thus forces us to be proactive instead of reactive. The only way to be proactive is to force ourselves to take time to think ahead. That's the only way to get to formation on time. It's the only way to win a battle. It's the only way to lead a successful company. To sit and think takes discipline. The pressure of accountability should force that discipline.

Think of Time in Seconds

"The difference between a good and a great officer is about ten seconds," said Adm. Arleigh Burke, Chief of Naval Operations. "Time is of the essence," say most legal contracts.

Ten seconds at sea can be the difference between a decision that wins a battle or a failure to decide and losing it. Making a quick decision is important, but just as important is knowing the decision may need to be made and thus preparing to make it. The pressure of accountability makes the captain move quickly in thinking, preparing, and deciding. This pressure can exist ashore as well as at sea.

"I didn't have enough time" should seldom be a response to a poor decision.

Make Training the Backbone of Our Accountability

"How could you be so stupid?" yelled the chief petty officer. I was a young ensign just starting my first job as a division officer in charge of thirty deck seamen. The chief went on to blast the poor seaman apprentice for not swabbing (mopping) the deck correctly. The sailor had wet the swab, never rinsing it, and brushed back and forth over the deck, effectively spreading the dirt evenly across the deck.

I learned a lesson then that I tried to remember the rest of my career. Had anyone trained the sailor in how to swab a deck correctly? Maybe the fault was not with the seaman apprentice but with the chief who did not train the sailor in the first place. Training, I learned, was the key to successful performance—my training and the training of my crew.

A personal attitude of accountability may not be possible unless we understand that training ourselves and our employees is our responsibility. If we want to have employees we can hold accountable, we must first train ourselves and our employees.

Be Ready to Take Control

"Captain has the conn!" I yelled. We were alongside an oiler, refueling at sea. The replenishment ship had lost steering control, and the ships were separated by only 120 feet and moving at twelve knots.

While generally a junior officer under my watchful eye had the conn (the designation of the only person who can give the helmsman an order), in an emergency I wanted direct control of the ship.

While alarms were sounding and emergency breakaway procedures were in place, I made adjustments to our course to keep us from colliding with the other ship. Experience had taught me to look aft (backward) as much as forward in case the sterns of the ships moved together while everyone was looking forward. In less than a minute our fueling hoses had been disconnected, and we were gradually able to work our way clear of the out-of-control replenishment ship until it was able to stop. I gave the conn back to the officer of the deck.

Whether at sea or ashore, leaders always need to be ready to take control when necessary. Often only one person—ourself—is in a position to effectively handle a crisis, whether one of life or death or one of business success.

Holding ourselves accountable means we have spent time thinking about potential challenges, training ourselves to handle them, and then taking personal charge when required. In any organization crisis, the leader's standing in front of the cameras saying what he or she is doing about the crisis instills confidence in everyone else. The leader stands in front of the cameras because the leader knows he or she is responsible for whatever happens.

Accountability Prevents Chaos

"Who's in charge here? . . . Abandon ship!" I imagine the people on the first boat ever to go to sea thousands of years ago asked that question as their boat was sinking. They all looked around and found no one was in charge, and so they abandoned ship as it sank. Some survivors made it ashore. After gaining a new appreciation for dry land, the next time they went to sea, they appointed a leader, who was called captain. Most ships since have not had to abandon ship.

But if they did abandon ship, now they had someone to blame if the ship sank. More important, they had someone who could prevent the ship from sinking. They had someone who took accountability for keeping the ship and crew safe. Captains ever since have refined their leadership techniques for keeping the ship afloat.

We wouldn't think much progress has been made when watching the movie *Titanic* or reading about the grounding of the cruise ship *Costa Concordia* or more recently a Korean ferry. The captains in those catastrophes should not have been captains. They had lost their sense of accountability. If they hadn't, they would not have allowed circumstances to sink their ships, their crews would have been trained in how to abandon ship effectively, or they would not have blamed someone else for the sinking.

On one of my early ships, as a division officer, my captain explained to me after watching another ship bump the pier because it was going too fast: "No captain is a complete failure. He can always serve as a bad example."

Ships sink and organizations ultimately fail when leaders have no sense of personal accountability. Using a sea captain's mental attitude of accountability can create a unique pressure to focus any leader on his or her leadership style and thus be ready for a Hobson's choice.

Discussion and Reflection Questions

1. Do you see the responsibilities of your job as much broader than just your job description?
2. Do you feel the pressure of total accountability for your decisions and those of your employees? What about those of your boss?
3. Do you feel accountable for the success of your business or organization or is that someone else's job?
4. What key decisions do you make? What key decisions does your boss make?
5. Are you training yourself to make your boss' decisions some day?
6. What are you doing differently from your peers to accelerate your career?
7. Who do you blame if you are not being promoted? What are you doing about it?

"I'll Find Out, Sir!"
Thinking and Learning Leadership

CNN Television Control Room. (Courtesy of CNN)

November 1942

After their victory at Pearl Harbor, Japan's military forces were capturing island after island in the South Pacific as they moved toward the coast of Australia. The Allies decided to reverse the Japanese advance with an attack on the island of Guadalcanal. In early 1942, after a successful landing, U.S. Marines engaged in a desperate struggle to maintain their foothold on the island. Japanese forces were being constantly resupplied from Rabaul to the north. The U.S. Navy was tasked with intercepting these supply ships.

On November 25, 1942, fleet commander Adm. Bull Halsey ordered Capt. Arleigh Burke, famous for high-speed tactics, to intercept a Japanese convoy sailing for Guadalcanal: "31 Knot Burke, get this: Put your squadron athwart the Buka–Rabaul line . . . if any enemy contacted, you know what to do."

Burke immediately got under way with a squadron of five destroyers and, since he could not patrol every course the Japanese might take, decided to operate near Cape St. George. During the night he found the Japanese group and quickly sank two ships. While pursuing the other ships in the convoy, he lost sight of them in the dark but kept a course he thought would allow his squadron to intercept them.

His ships had been steaming in a column on this course for a few minutes when he decided something was wrong. He barked the following order: "All ships, immediate execute, turn starboard 45, standby, execute." At the order "execute," all his ships started turning at the same time to a new course forty-five degrees to the right of the previous one.

Suddenly massive explosions erupted in the wakes of his squadron ships. The Japanese had spotted Burke's destroyers and had fired a spread of long-range torpedoes, which exploded where his ships would have been if they had not turned. Burke's immediate-execute decision saved his squadron from being sunk and allowed it to proceed to sink or damage the rest of the Japanese force in one of the earliest U.S. Navy victories in World War II.

Knowing What to Do

How did Halsey know that Burke knew what to do? He didn't give detailed orders. Why Burke knew what to do is the subject of this chapter.

On a Navy ship, there is only one chair on the bridge, the captain's chair. Everyone else stands during their four-hour watches. Only the captain, who may be on the bridge through many watches, has a chair. It's there because the captain spends a lot of time watching, listening, and thinking. The captain is constantly thinking about decisions he or she may need to make and what can go wrong in the next few minutes or days.

August 1991

The USS *O'Brien* was entering the port of Abu Dhabi with visibility limited to a mile, the low seawall hard to detect on radar, unreliable navigation aids, and no harbor pilot available. That makes the ship navigator's job tough.

I had been sitting in the Captain's chair, listening to the navigator's verbal reports to the bridge team. They went something like this: "Officer of the deck, based on a good fix, I hold the ship on track. Nearest shoal water is five hundred yards off the port bow. Nearest navigation aid is buoy seven off the port bow. Next turn will be to starboard in six minutes to course 265. Recommend maintaining course and speed."

"Very well," replied the officer of the deck. It's important for the navigator to know his report was heard by the officer conning (giving orders to the helmsman) the ship.

Suddenly the navigator reported, "Poor fix time 0715. Based on estimated position, hold the ship on track. Recommend slowing speed to five knots." The officer of the deck slowed the ship.

"Poor fix time 0716," was the next report. "Based on estimated position, hold the ship on track. Next turn will be to starboard to course 265 in eight minutes." (The ship had slowed.)

I was looking at the breakwater off the starboard side and comparing my thinking about the ship's position with what I was hearing. I had studied the charts carefully the night before.

Something wasn't right. There were two entrances to the harbor. Both were hard to see in the haze. The second entrance was too shallow for the ship, so entering through the first was the only option. I had taken note of some tall towers on the other side of the harbor that were visually aligned with the first harbor entrance. I saw that the towers were now aligned; it was time to turn the ship.

If the navigation team thought there was another few minutes until the turn, they obviously were not plotting the ship's real position. We were in danger of running aground within a minute.

"Captain has the conn!" I said loudly so there was no confusion to the helmsman. "Right full rudder, all engines back full." The ship swung to the right and stopped. We were now pointed in the right direction.

"Officer of the deck has the conn," I ordered.

"I have the conn," he replied, looking a little relieved that the ship was still afloat. A crisis had been averted and his career was still there. So was mine. We proceeded into port.

What went wrong? Me. While sitting in the captain's chair the previous day I had studied the two entries and could tell by the structures on either side which was which. While our navigation brief with the watch team had mentioned the second entrance, the brief had not focused as much as it should have on what we would do if visibility was bad and radar returns were poor.

As a team we did not think ahead very well, and the fault was mine. As the most experienced officer on board, I should have made sure we discussed better what could go wrong. We tried not to make that mistake again.

But I did what a captain or any leader is supposed to do during critical events: listen, think, and act if necessary. Listening was key. When the navigator reported "no fix," my thinking about what could go wrong went into gear. I was not involved in the details of the ship's operations from the bridge; I was detached, focusing only on the ship's position. I was not automatically following the navigator's recommendations.

Because I was listening, thinking ahead with the view of what can go wrong, noticing when it did go wrong, and then taking action, we did not run aground. But the fact that we got into this situation was my fault. We should have thought ahead as a team better. I was responsible for making sure that happened.

Arleigh Burke thought ahead. As a result, he won one of the key surface-ship-only battles of World War II. Why did he win this key battle and why did I recover in the nick of time from not fully preparing my team for entering a strange port?

The answers to these questions lie in the "I'll find out" leadership trait of ship captains. "I'll find out" means thinking ahead and learning what we need to know, knowing what homework we need to do, and thinking about what to do before we need to do it. We can call that "I'll find out" leadership. Burke had thought about patrol areas in advance; he had thought about what could go wrong when faced with superior Japanese torpedoes. I had done my own homework on entering the Abu Dhabi port, but I had not shared that thinking with my team.

"Finding Out" Leadership by
Thinking Ahead and Learning

August 2011

I dropped by the CNN control room after lunch on August 23, 2011, to see what was going on in Libya. As a frequent military commentator at CNN, I tried to stay current on military-related events. The executive producer of the on-air show suggested I stick around since after a two-minute commercial break they were going live to Nick Roberts, who was broadcasting from Muammar Gaddafi's captured headquarters in Tripoli.

With about ninety seconds left in the break, an assistant producer in the back of the control room called out that she had viewed a tweet from a friend in Martha's Vineyard stating an earthquake had just hit there. A few seconds later another producer announced she had just seen a tweet from a friend in Roanoke, Virginia, that an earthquake had hit there too.

With about sixty seconds to go before going live, the executive producer calmly set in motion actions to confirm and then go live with the story. Assistant producers were assigned to contact the Washington and New York CNN bureaus (Washington called a few seconds later) and get CNN's weather team to confirm the quake, and the on-air anchor was notified of the potential breaking news. The main CNN newsroom automatically jumped into action to support the on-air team in the control room.

With confirmation from the Washington bureau that there had been a significant earthquake, the executive producer ordered the Libya story on hold and told the anchor everything the team had learned about the quake. CNN went live with a breaking news story that had developed over ninety seconds. Anchors really make their living in situations like this, where there is little initial news but a confirmed breaking story.

After a brief live take of the anchor, the executive producer put on air a live camera shot of the White House; CNN always has a live picture of the White House on a monitor in the control room. Wolf Blitzer was in Washington and called in for an audio report within a minute of CNN's reporting the story. Within minutes CNN cameras were on the roof of the bureau, showing people evacuating buildings around Capitol Hill.

All of this was taking place without detailed orders to each location on what to do.

There was no time to think in the control room at 1:51 on August 23, but there had been a lot of thinking, planning, and practicing of responses to breaking news events such as this one. The executive producer was prepared to make a quick decision without a lot of information. She did not have to get permission to change the broadcast plan. Her decisions had the air of calm confidence. In a way, the CNN response that day was like Arleigh Burke's response to Halsey's order: "You know what to do." The CNN team did know what to do, and they did an immediate execute.

"Finding out" leadership of thinking ahead and learning can be divided into two categories: routine and special. In the Navy, routine decisions made in advance are often put in the standing orders of a captain. This document contains the preplanned orders of the captain to his or her watch teams if the captain is not present on the bridge.

These orders cover actions like how close the officer of the deck can pass another ship to when the tactical action officer—on his or her own command—can quickly fire a missile in defense of the ship. Because the captain has thought ahead about what routine decisions might need to be made, the captain and the crew know what to do in certain situations. Because early thought is given about the routine decisions, and directions are put in writing in advance, few mistakes are made.

But there is no useful way to put in writing everything than can happen or go wrong. We need to be ready to suddenly respond to events like torpedoes, getting lost while entering port, or reporting an earthquake. In these cases, we find out what the challenges might be and prepare to handle them when there is not much time to think.

At sea, there are dozens of things that could go wrong every day, but they don't all go wrong. You never hear about instances that could have been disasters had the captain not thought about his or her decisions in advance. If captains don't think ahead, disasters like the *Titanic* happen. Think ahead, and potential disasters like Burke's squadron being sunk by torpedoes don't happen.

Thinking ahead is just as important for an organization. We live in an era where very different generations are now in the workplace: Boomers, Gen Ys, and Gen Xs. Each of these generations has unique characteristics. For instance, Gen Xs are much more casual, much more technology-oriented, and much more likely as parents to work outside of their home. Put them all together, and we have a situation like mooring a ship, where the needs and wants of clients are changing like the tides and winds. Business leaders need to think about what decisions they need to make to keep their business relevant to the changing demographics.

Think ahead, and we can be ready to respond to a breakdown in the production line. Thinking ahead and thinking about what can go wrong are the foundations of thinking like ship captains. Both are necessary to be ready to know what to do. To be ready, captains have an "I'll find out" mentality.

"Finding Out" Leadership Means "What Can Go Wrong?" Thinking

When an amphibious landing, like that on D-day in World War II, is made, the ships supporting the assault are all combat loaded. That means that critical supplies of one type are not all loaded on one ship; they are stored in several ships. The Navy and Marines do that because if one ship carrying all the tanks is sunk, the Marines charging ashore would be without a key element of support. Better to have a few tanks than none.

Losing all the tanks at the same time does not happen because someone gave some thought as to what might go wrong. My wife has kindly put up with my insistence that when we travel together, we put our clothes in both suitcases in case one gets lost. Of course, we have never lost a suitcase . . . yet.

Recently, Carnival Cruise Lines had a series of fires or mechanical failures on some of its ships. Loss of power on cruise liners should never happen if someone thinks about what can go wrong during design or operation. In Navy ships, generators are placed in compartments as far apart as possible. The thinking is that if the ship takes a hit or has a fire in one generator room, the others can still operate. In the design and operation of cruise ships, there was apparently a lack of thinking about what could go wrong.

Organization leaders ashore should also approach decisions with additional thoughts of what might go wrong. My experience has been that most things in organizations go wrong because of a lack of communication. Someone never got informed, someone could not contact someone, someone didn't show up on time (a problem on television), etc. Spending time thinking about what can go wrong will allow decision makers to be proactive instead of reactive when things do not go as planned. Communication is generally what goes wrong the most.

How to Create "I'll Find Out" Leadership to Think Ahead and Learn

The Houston ship channel is the most hair-raising port approach in the world. I have been in and out of many ports, but for sheer terror, career reviewing, and "this can't possibly work" excitement, nothing beats the Houston ship channel past Galveston.

The channel is not very wide. Supertankers are very wide. There is not much room left for a Navy cruiser. Two ships passing in opposite directions have a set series of procedures. First, they head right at each other in the center of the channel because there is not much room on either side. At this point I am telling myself there is no way we are not going to collide. The pilot, however, doesn't think much of it.

Second, at one mile, which when looking at the bow of a massive supertanker is not very far, each ship puts its rudder to the right for a few seconds and then turns it back left. That allows the ships to sashay around each other, passing not more than a few dozen yards apart. I can almost read the name tags on the tanker crew's uniforms.

Third, the captain says a prayer of thanks for deliverance, and then sees another supertanker ahead.

The channel is not very wide because it must be constantly dredged to keep sand from filling up the middle. At one point I looked down at a navigation marker ten yards off the side of the ship to see a guy fishing next to the marker . . . he was standing in the water! My ship needed thirty feet of water to float.

I asked the pilot if passing ships brushed against the sides of the channel.

"Frequently," he replied. Seeing my eyes get big, he added, "But don't worry, since the sides are sand, we would just bounce off."

"Sir," I replied, "in the United States Navy, when we bounce off something, we call that 'running aground' and the captain gets a new job in Kansas."

He smiled. We entered the port safely. The procedure to pass in the narrow channel had had a lot of thought given to it.

As leaders, we know we need to think ahead. We need to do it, but often we don't. So how do we better motivate ourselves to create a find-out mentality of thinking ahead like a ship captain? Here are some suggestions.

Have a Reminder to Think Ahead

There is no way for a captain to sneak on or off the ship. When I crossed the brow onto the ship, the quarterdeck watch rang four bells on the general ship sound system and announced, "*Cape St. George*, arriving." The flag that indicated I was off the ship was hauled down. The watch standers all came to attention.

Note that when the captain is arriving or departing, the quarterdeck watch does not announce "the boss is here" or use the captain's name. Instead it uses the ship's name. This tradition has a very definite point established over hundreds of years. It's not to create an inflated ego in the captain; it's to remind the captain that he or she is the one totally accountable for the ship and its crew. That mental attitude is the most fundamental requirement to be a captain or, in fact, to be a leader of any organization.

In businesses ashore, a leader does not get bells rung upon arrival at the office, but we should mentally pause each time we walk through the front door and remind ourselves that the company and its employees depend on us for its success and jobs. A mental sense of accountability will hopefully then be present during whatever the day ahead includes.

Create Thinking Pulse Points by Walking Around

My favorite indicator of how well the guns would shoot was the forward paint storage room. I had to climb down three decks on a vertical ladder, opening and closing watertight hatches as I went, look around, and then climb back up. It took about ten seconds of looking around to see if the guns would shoot straight.

If the paint locker, an out-of-the-way place, was neat and tidy, then the same professional mind-set of the crew would apply to more critical systems like the guns. It didn't hurt that the crew knew I checked the paint locker periodically; that meant the paint locker received their attention. That space was a *pulse point* as a reflection of the professionalism of the crew and the leadership holding them up.

Another favorite place for me to visit was the forward engine room late at night. There I could chat with the engineer on watch. In general conversation about his family, professional goals, or upcoming port visits, I could gauge his morale. Add to that conversation a few others in various parts of the ship at night, and I could get a sense of the overall morale of the ship. That morale could change quickly, so having frequent conversations was important. Talking with the crew was a pulse point for morale.

There were other pulse points, and the common thread in all of them was that I had to walk around the ship to take the pulse. I could not sit on my chair on the bridge to get a feel for what was going on in the rest of the ship.

As I walked around, I was reminded that all the spaces I visited and all the crew members I met were all my responsibility. If the forward paint storage area was a mess, it was my responsibility not only to make sure it was cleaned up but also to see what professional attitude I needed to inspire so it stayed clean. Just getting it cleaned once was not the final solution.

Finding solutions to reinforce good performance or correcting underperforming areas required knowing about the performance and then finding a solution. Business leaders can't lead from their offices either.

Take Notice of Family Pictures on Employee Desks

A sailor does not have much space to store clothes and other personal items. Each sailor gets a small vertical locker and a storage box underneath the mattress. That's it. With maybe thirty other sailors living in the same space, there is not much room for storage.

When I walked around the ship and visited the berthing areas, I would chat with sailors with their storage boxes open and some family pictures taped to the inside lid. Those pictures were a great source of conversation. I liked to see a picture of a daughter playing soccer or the sailor and his wife on their honeymoon. Everyone wants to talk about their families.

To me, seeing the pictures was a rewarding part of the job of being captain, but they also reminded me of my total accountability for making sure the sailor got home safely. That sailor had a family who depended on him or her. And the sailor's family depended on me. I was accountable for making sure mom got home to watch a soccer game or that a husband returned home to his new bride.

As business leaders, we know we should always work to take care of our employees. How important is that duty? All we have to do is look at the pictures on desks or bulletin boards to realize that the livelihood and productive lives of our employees and their families are our responsibility as leaders. We must remember we are accountable for entire families when we see their pictures on desks and walls when we walk around, but we must walk around to see them. There is no greater burden of accountability than families, ours and our employees.

Always Be Thinking, What Can Go Wrong?

In July 1967, the USS *Forrestal* was conducting flight operations in the Gulf of Tonkin off the coast of Vietnam. While aircraft were getting ready to launch, a power surge in one of the aircraft caused a rocket to fire across the deck, hitting another aircraft armed with bombs and carrying external fuel tanks. The tanks ruptured, the fuel ignited, and the bombs dropped to the deck in the burning fuel and exploded.

A trained firefighting team was moving into position when the bombs exploded, wiping out the team. Other aircraft and munitions exploded over the next few minutes, putting the ship in danger of sinking. Heroic efforts by the crew and airmen kept the ship afloat, but in the end 134 sailors were killed and 167 were injured. The carrier was out of action for almost a year.

The fire and the firefighting efforts were all captured by video cameras that all carriers use to monitor flight deck operations. Given the magnitude of the disaster, a training film was made of the video and has ever since been shown to every sailor in the Navy. It shows heroism, a lack of training, and a lack of thinking ahead.

Several books have been written about the accident, but there are a few key lessons that can be learned. Safety procedures for ensuring munitions don't accidentally fire were not followed. Many munitions were not made to withstand fire for ten minutes; they exploded in less than two minutes. No one had thought about what to do if the primary firefighting team was lost while battling a shipboard fire. No one had thought about training the entire crew in firefighting. Hosing down burning fuel into the flight deck only made the fire worse inside the ship.

A lot of thought and planning has since been done on flight deck firefighting. The flight deck can now be automatically coated in foam. All sailors get firefighting training. Safety procedures are meticulously followed. Ordnance can now withstand fire for much longer times. And captains now make sure the training and procedures are done correctly.

The *Forrestal* fire is an example of not enough thought being given to what can go wrong. It's also an example of how previous thought can be lost due to intense operations exerting pressure on performance. It's an example ships at sea and organizations and companies ashore can use to remind ourselves to be constantly thinking about what can go wrong. When we do that, fewer things go wrong. Fires don't happen, competitive edges are maintained, laws are not broken, budgets balance, and people are better trained.

Think Forward but Look Astern

Nothing looks worse in ship handling when mooring to a pier than to have the bow of the ship next to the pier with the stern hanging out in the channel like laundry. Crew members on other ships might remark that it looked like the ship's cooks were maneuvering the ship. There's nothing wrong with cooks conning the ship, if they are trained to do so.

I'd teach young officers that when mooring a ship without the assistance of tugboats, they needed to look aft as much as they looked forward. Seeing what the winds, currents, and past course changes were doing to the entire ship—not just the bow—was important. The same is true whenever we are thinking ahead. We must keep in mind what mistakes have happened in the past (I bumped the pier several times by going too fast), not dump traditions too fast (there is a reason why the tradition exists), and see how our previous actions affect where we are going.

"Finding out" leadership means thinking ahead and learning, but it also means finding out about the past. There are reasons why companies are where they are today. Some are very good reasons.

Think Ahead about Careers, Our Employees, and Our Own

Ships that are tops in the fleet for retention are allowed to paint their anchors gold. Gold anchors really stand out on an otherwise gray ship and generally indicate a good ship. If I were the enemy and knew I was going up against a gold anchor ship, I'd go the other way.

Gold anchors do not come easy. They don't just happen. They happen because the crew knows their personal career plans as well as the ship's operational plans.

Late at night, while roaming the ship and talking to the younger crew members, I'd often ask, "So what's your career plan?" Having planned mine from my days at the Naval Academy, I was always surprised how many sailors had given it little thought. When I asked where they wanted to be in their careers five or ten years down the road, I'd often get a blank stare. They weren't even sure they wanted to be in the Navy.

Career advice needs to be personal. Young employees or crew members need help thinking through career plans. Where do they want to go? What training do they need to get there? Good ships have personal plans for everyone. Competitive companies need such planning too.

Leaders should also be looking constantly at our own careers. Are we on track? Are we constantly learning? Are we satisfied with our chosen profession? These are good topics for thought during the time we set aside to think.

One thing I learned about gold anchor ships: If a sailor decided to leave the Navy, the chain of command would do everything possible to assist that sailor in his or her new line of work, such as writing letters of recommendation. Interestingly, once the crew knows the captain will do things like write letters of recommendation to civilian companies, fewer sailors on that ship decide to leave the Navy.

Set Aside a Place and Time to Think

On the ship, I needed a place to think that was not just my chair on the bridge. My favorite place was the main deck while I jogged lap after lap during lunchtime. The deck might be flat, but with rolling or pitching, there was enough going up and down that it seemed like the deck had hills. On the narrow sections where steel doors opened out on the deck, I'd have to jog by with my hands out in front in case someone opened the door at the wrong time. A ship captain cannot look dashing with a broken nose.

We all need to have a place and set time to think. Jogging at sea was my place on the ship and jogging on a quiet road was my place ashore. My experience is that having a set location that is special to thinking and a set time just to think is critical to the "finding out" leadership of thinking ahead. Thinking has to be proactive, not reactive.

Always Have a Plan

"I'm caught between the devil and the deep blue sea" is said by those who find themselves in a situation where they have to make a choice between two undesirable outcomes. Few people know it's a naval term that does not refer to Satan in the boiling heat of the underworld.

The "devil" on old sailing ships was the outermost seam of the wooden planks where the deck met the hull. The seam was the hardest to caulk, so it was called the devil. To caulk it, a sailor had to hang precariously out over the side of the ship and would often get caught by high waves. Thus to be "between the devil and the deep blue sea" was not an enviable position.

In today's business environment, we can easily be placed in a position where we are between the devil and the deep blue sea. We generally get in trouble, or don't meet expectations, because we don't have a plan.

In the Navy, there is a plan for most everything: plan of the day, plan of the week, training plan, maintenance plan, replenishment plan, meal plan, man overboard plan, liberty plan, etc. Plans mean we have thought ahead about how to best respond to known challenges and needs.

Companies need plans just like the Navy: financial plans, business plans, promotion plans, tax plans, etc. To have "find out" mentality, leaders need to create plans that address many known future events or avoid making the same past mistakes.

Failure to have a plan means there may be the devil to pay. On sailing ships of yore, that meant caulking the devil, which was often a punishment detail. Crew members would tell a mate who had broken some ship rule that he would "have the devil to pay." Planning is a key to good leadership, and thinking ahead is the only way to correctly plan.

Arleigh Burke thought ahead, developed options, chose one, and was always thinking about what could go wrong. He thought this way because he held himself accountable. In the effort to develop options, he had to plan how to learn about the options and how he would execute the one he chose. Thinking ahead and learning like ship captains is a step in deciding like them.

Discussion and Reflection Questions

1. What is your job description? Do you feel accountable for the decisions your boss or others in your organization make?
2. Do you set aside time to think?
3. Do you spend time walking around watching and listening?
4. What can go wrong in your job today? In the next few weeks?
5. What is your plan to not let things go wrong?
6. Do you have a list of key decisions you must make in the near and long term?

5

"Yes/No, Sir!"
Ethical Leadership

Costa Concordia on its side off Isola del Giglio, Tuscany. (Wikimedia Commons/paolodefalco75)

February 1996

"Attention on deck!" the master-at-arms commands as I walk into the room.

This is a captain's mast. Coming to attention are the officers, petty officers, and witnesses in the case of a sailor who has violated a regulation in the Uniform Code of Military Justice (UCMJ). In this case, a seaman was caught sleeping on watch.

Though not a court-martial, a captain's mast is still a serious disciplinary event. As captain, I can award various levels of penalties, including reduction in pay grades, fines up to a certain amount, restriction to the ship, and even bread and water for three days in the brig (jail). Courts-martial are for serious violations and can result in much more severe punishments. On a ship, the captain is both judge and jury. To make the system work, the Navy and the ship's crew must trust the captain's judgment.

The master-at-arms calls in the accused. "Uncover," he commands. The accused takes off his hat. I have my hat on. It's a symbol of authority now readily noticeable, like a judge wearing a black robe.

I read to him the article of the UCMJ he is accused of violating and read him his rights. Next, I have the witnesses explain what happened. They say he was asleep while on watch in the after steering room. This is a critical watch, as he is responsible for steering the ship from direct control of the rudders should normal steering be lost in the pilothouse. It is a watch that is always manned when the ship is under way. Sleeping on this watch could endanger the ship if steering were suddenly lost at a critical moment.

After hearing the witnesses, I ask the accused for his response to the charges. "Yes, sir," he says. "I did fall asleep, sir. But it was only for a few minutes, sir."

I am glad he said "yes" to my question. I'm not sure how long a "few minutes" might be. One minute is too long. I turn to his chain of command for comments on how good a worker and shipmate the seaman has been since he reported on board a few months ago.

His division chief petty officer comments: "Excellent worker, Captain. We can trust him to do what he is assigned to do. He has, however, been late to muster a few times over the past few weeks."

"Why is that?" I ask the seaman.

"I didn't hear reveille, so I didn't get out of my rack in time, sir."

I ask him a few more questions, mostly focused on what recently was causing him to oversleep. I want to know if he is being assigned jobs that severely limit his time to rest or if he was just getting sloppy with his duties. He admits to not focusing more on his jobs.

Time for my judgment and, if necessary, punishment. Here is basically a good sailor, liked by his shipmates, who does his assigned work. He has not been to captain's mast since reporting on board, but he is starting to lose his credibility and has violated a key safety rule. Time to get his attention. Also time to show the rest of the crew that sleeping on watch is a serious safety violation.

"I find you guilty as charged," I announce. "I assign you the punishment of reduction in rate to seaman apprentice, restriction to the ship during our next port call, and extra duty for one week. However, due to your good work performance I am suspending your reduction in rate for one month. If you do not violate another regulation during that period, you will remain a seaman. Shipmates must trust their fellow shipmates to stand their watches correctly. Without that trust, this ship cannot operate. Can I trust you that this will not happen again?"

"Yes, sir!" The seaman looks relieved that he has not been reduced in grade. I hope he has learned his lesson.

"Dismissed," I order. The master-at-arms marches him out of the room.

Why do we need to know about a captain's mast? There are several reasons:

- It shows that a set of rules and standards is necessary for a ship to function at sea. The same is true for a business ashore, even if the disciplinary action is not the same.
- It shows that crew members depend on all other shipmates to do their jobs, and if one doesn't, there is order and discipline that will protect the rest of the crew.
- It shows that when a question is answered truthfully ("I did fall asleep"), discipline can be less severe and thus a lesson to others.
- It shows there is right and wrong conduct.
- It shows that honestly answering questions with a "yes" or "no" is at the core of ethics.

Yes or No: Two Small Words with Huge Meaning

Saying truthfully "yes, sir" or "no, sir" when asked a question is a lesson taught in the first sixty seconds at the Naval Academy. It's a sudden, very real test of honesty, character, and the degree of trust someone can place on the person answering the question. "Did you polish your shoes this morning?" Say "yes" and it's proven you didn't, you could be dismissed from the academy. If you can't be trusted to truthfully answer a question about shining your shoes, why should someone trust you to command a ship?

Yes and *no* are two small words that have huge meanings. They can represent our personal understanding of right and wrong. Answering a question with an honest "yes" or "no" is the foundation of a personal code of ethics. And it is our personal code of ethics that creates trust.

Answering honestly is often not that easy. Many times we are deciding between telling the truth or lying. We only have a second to answer, and that is not much time to think about right and wrong. This is why ship captains need a personal code of ethics wherein they have taken time to think about their concept of right and wrong before facing a question or event requiring an ethical response.

In short, how we answer a question tells us a lot about our character.

Twenty-First-Century Trust: Believing Yes and No Answers

New York Times columnist David Brooks recently wrote an op-ed titled "New Trust Calculus Fuels Peer-to-Peer Economy." He makes the interesting observation that while people have lost trust in big institutions like corporations and government, there has arisen a new "personalistic" culture where social trust is growing between individuals.

Airbnb is a peer-to-peer website that links people who want to rent a private home to those who are looking for one. The homeowners are willing to rent to and trust strangers. Eleven million people stayed in Airbnb destinations last year.

Many of us check reviews of hotels or cruise ships on websites like Trip Advisor to see what the real truth is about a location. A company website is not fully trusted. We do trust fellow travelers to answer honestly a question like "Would you recommend this location to a friend?" We trust the opinions of strangers.

But who are our popular role models for trust? Here is the *Reader's Digest* list of the most trusted people in the United States: Tom Hanks, Sandra Bullock, Denzel Washington, Meryl Streep, and Maya Angelou. Not one leader of an organization was listed. Here are some other notables in the top one hundred on the list: (7) Bill Gates, (32) Colin Powell, (65) Barack Obama, and (71) Warren Buffett.

Most of the list includes actors, film producers, talk show hosts, news anchors, and, thankfully, Supreme Court justices. Falling toward the bottom of the list are a few business leaders: Jeff Bezos of Amazon, Alex Gorsky of Johnson and Johnson, and Steve Forbes.

A Gallup poll reports that Americans trust the following professions:

Nurses (82 percent)
Pharmacists (70 percent)
Grade school teachers (70 percent)
Medical doctors (69 percent)
Military officers (69 percent)

Other notable professions have the following levels of trust:

Bankers (27 percent)
Local officials (23 percent)
Business executives (22 percent)
Lawyers (20 percent)
Car salesmen (9 percent)
U.S. Congress (8 percent)

I find it interesting that the most trusted people in America are actors and actresses, but the most trusted professions are related to health and education. There were no nurses listed in the *Reader's Digest* poll. Only one military officer (Colin Powell) was named. Out of one hundred people, the only politicians were President Obama and former president Jimmy Carter.

The approval rating for Congress was at the bottom of the list at 8 percent. Yet every two years Americans re-elect more than 90 percent of the incumbents. Except for Bill Gates, all the business leaders who are responsible for people were in the bottom quarter of the list.

Trust in the twenty-first century seems to be a changing and confusing term. Business organizations and governments no longer have the respect of most people, but people still seem to trust people, even those they do not know.

Trust has not, however, changed in meaning for centuries and is not a confusing term to the crew on a ship. Trust is and always has been about people. It has always been necessary to have trust up and down the chain of command. Successful ships thrive on trust. Creating trust in the current business environment ashore can lead to success too.

Trust: A Military *and* Business Competitive Edge

An interesting difference between the Soviet navy and the U.S. Navy during the Cold War era was that each Soviet ship had at least one political officer on board who did not report to the captain. His job was to observe and report to organizations like the KGB any suspicious conduct or attitudes by crew members or officers. The Soviet government did not trust its sailors, and their performance was degraded because of it.

Shortly after the unification of Germany in 1990, I had the opportunity to visit a Soviet tank company in East Berlin. Their barracks looked like our barracks. Their tanks looked ready to roll. During lunch with the company commander, however, he told me that they were always ready to attack, but he felt they would only be able to go a few miles.

"Why is that?" I asked, expecting him to say that Allied defenses would stop them.

His answer was surprising. "We believed we could overrun the defenses if we made a surprise attack, but we would never get far because our commanders had no trust in our units. We almost had to ask permission to shift from first gear to second gear. We had no authority to be flexible."

The U.S. Navy, on the other hand, depends entirely on the trust it gives to commanding officers and the crews of ships. Flexibility to adapt to changing circumstances has always been an option given to captains. Trust is a competitive edge our Navy enjoys over most all other navies in the world.

So in an era of diminishing trust of businesses and governments, creating trust between employees and customers can be a significant competitive edge for businesses. Developing an organization that can be trusted and then selling that trust along with a product is exactly what ship captains have been doing for centuries, except that the product is successfully accomplishing a mission.

When we buy homes, it's the agent we trust, not the realty company. When we bank, with rates for loans and savings much the same everywhere, it's the banker we want to trust for advice, not the bank. When you are a crew member, it's the captain you want to trust. The need for trust is the same. And creating trust is the same too.

Creating Trust

A guided missile cruiser in the U.S. Navy has a crew of about five hundred, including an aviation department that operates two helicopters. The ship is about five hundred feet long and fifty feet wide. That's not much space for that many sailors (though better than World War II–era light cruisers, which had more than a thousand crew members). As a result, everyone knows everyone intimately, and the families ashore get to know other ship families too. It's a tight community in a large Navy. Trust is hard to earn and easy to lose in this type of environment. Trust is something that is person to person, as it is becoming in the twenty-first century everywhere.

The days of command like those of Captain William Bligh and the mutiny on the HMS *Bounty* are long gone. The days when a captain did not need to have his crew's trust to effectively command are over, if they ever existed. It's not just blind discipline anymore. A captain today only gives orders the captain knows will be obeyed, and they will be obeyed because of discipline and the trust a crew has in the captain's judgment. A captain earns the trust of the crew in the same way a business executive earns it in any organization: personal job competence, a code of ethics, and an understanding that the same ethics that apply at sea apply ashore as well (in the office and out of the office).

1. Achieve Personal Job Competence

"Man overboard! Starboard side!" yelled the port-side lookout shortly after I had taken command of the USS *Cape St. George*. The standard procedures were immediately taken by the officer of the deck.

"Right standard rudder!" he commanded. "Sound six blasts on the ship's whistle! Petty officer of the watch, pass the word on the announcing system." Right full rudder was ordered to get the stern of the ship and the propellers away from the person in the water. Six blasts on the ship's whistle is the international signal of an emergency and for other ships to stand clear.

"Man overboard, starboard side!" the petty officer of the watch announced to the crew on the ship-wide sound system. Like battle stations, most of the crew members have specific assignments: deck sailors raced to the lifeboats, ready to lower them to pick up the sailor in the water; other sailors raced to the forward part of the ship with lifelines ready to throw if the ship came alongside the sailor; lookouts pointed continuously to the sailor in the water to make sure visual contact was not lost; the entire crew held a muster to get the name of the person in the water.

"This is the captain, I have the conn," I announced on the bridge. At any time a ship is under way, only one person is allowed to give orders to the helmsman.

"The captain has the conn," the officer of the deck replied.

"All engines ahead full, increase your rudder to right full," I ordered. "This will be a shipboard recovery." Due to the high sea state, I decided to bring the ship alongside the man in the water rather than risk putting a boat in the water.

The ship increases speed and turns sharply. I maneuver the ship, turning and then slowing so that it is parallel to the waves and winds and drifts down on the man in the water. The sailors on the forward part of the ship recover the dummy I had previously thrown in the water.

"Officer of the deck has the conn," I stated. I am transferring control back to him.

"I have the conn," he replied.

It was a drill for the ship, and for me. I wanted to show the crew that I knew how to maneuver the ship. I wanted them to gain trust in me for ship handling. There were a lot of other areas I needed to equally earn their professional trust, but this was one of the most important.

I had learned ship handling over the years as an officer on various ships. I worked at it, mainly because I really enjoyed maneuvering ten thousand tons of ship. Over the years I also made sure I served in every department on a warship: weapons, operations, engineering, and navigation. I wanted to learn the basics so I could be an effective captain at some point in the future. When I finally took command, I knew I still had a lot to learn, but I felt confident in knowing the basics. That gave me some confidence. It hopefully gave the crew some trust in my job competence.

Business leaders can start to gain the trust of their employees by making sure they know the basics of their business too. Knowing all the procedures, the organizational structure, the equipment, the potential problems, and the opportunities will instill confidence and trust not only in themselves but also in their employees.

Young managers can create trust immediately by taking time to learn the basics of their job descriptions. Following that, they can further enhance the trust of their coworkers and bosses by learning how to handle the job descriptions of their peers. They should also be learning how to perform their boss' job. When he or she gets promoted, we should all want to be at the head of the line as a replacement.

For older managers, learning never ends. Things change: business environment, customers, regulations, our own qualifications. Employees expect a boss to know more or at least as much as they do. We need to make sure we meet those expectations.

2. Create a Personal Code of Ethics

He didn't have a sense of accountability and he didn't have a sense of ethics. He violated every rule in the book on being a captain. He was unable to answer the "yes" and "no" questions: Is it acceptable to depart from a planned ship track? Should I order abandon ship? Should I personally abandon ship when passengers and crew were still on board?

The captain of the *Costa Concordia*, Francesco Schettino, personally ran his ship with more than 3,200 passengers and crew on board— aground on January 13, 2012, off the coast of Italy near the town of Giglio Porto. He personally ordered a departure from the normal ship's track, without checking the charts, to show off his ship to passengers and people in the town.

The ship hit a rock, flooded, and sank next to the town. An abandon ship order was not made until about an hour after the ship started sinking. Thirty-two peopled died. It took more than six hours to evacuate the passengers and crew. It should have taken less than thirty minutes. With people still on the ship, Captain Schettino abandoned his ship and safely made it ashore.[1]

This incident has all types of examples of failures of accountability. The captain, obviously, but I would add the watch officers on the bridge at the time for not warning the captain or sending a distress radio call. I would add all the officers for not ensuring that the crew was proficient in assisting passengers in abandoning ship. I would add the owner of the ship, the Carnival Cruise line, for not ensuring the reliability of the officers or the correct training of the crew. Those are all obvious failures.

This incident also showed how the captain, the officers, and the crew all had a failure of character and ethics. They were not prepared to answer the simple questions about accountability and answer them truthfully. They had not thought through what was right and wrong in various situations, ranging from their jobs to their personal character.

Early in my career, a captain told me, "Always tell the truth, then you can always remember what you said." Another captain told his officers, "Never do anything that you would not want to see on the front page of the *Washington Post.*" Failures of ethics always appear on the front page of national newspapers. General David Petraeus is an unfortunate example. More on him later.

In an address to the U.S. Naval Academy, George Will commented, "Democracy does not encourage military values: trust, honor, teamwork, subordinating personal wants for the good of the whole." He went on to say that American society finds it hard to be judgmental, because passing judgment is considered one of the worst sins. One's rights override one's responsibilities. People can behave badly and not be judged harshly for it.

Earlier, I quoted a *Wall Street Journal* editorial: "Men will not long trust leaders who feel themselves beyond accountability for what they do. And when men lose confidence and trust . . . order disintegrates into chaos and purposeful ships into floating derelicts."

One of the greatest quotes about following a leader into danger are "I'd follow that man into hell if necessary." That leader has earned the trust of his subordinates. They know he can be trusted to do the right thing, give the right order, and treat his men fairly. He has earned their respect as well as their trust. Captains know the success and safety of their ship depends on the crew's trusting the captain and the captain's trusting the crew. The same is true in business too.

So if we realize that honesty and trust in a leader are so important to the success of any organization, why does it seem that few have developed a personal code of ethics or a business code of ethics? Too many leaders seem to end up on the front page of a newspaper for doing something illegal or something considered morally reprehensible.

In the fast-paced business and family environment today, there never seems to be enough time to stop and think about right and wrong or when to say "yes" and "no" honestly. If we weren't taught a sense of right and wrong early in life, developing that sense is not easy in an era where ethics are becoming increasingly relative.

A Navy ship captain has a set of regulations and directives that objectively provide what is authorized and what is not. There is, however, a lot of subjectivity in evaluating a captain's performance. Failure to create a command climate of trust and professionalism can result in a captain being relieved of his or her duties. A senior officer can lose confidence in a captain's ability to command for a number of subjective reasons. One of those is a lack of ethical conduct. So having a set of consciously developed ethics is a key to successfully commanding a ship.

Delta Airlines chairman and CEO Richard Anderson stated at a recent meeting that "only companies and countries with a sense of ethics last very long." Enron is a company that did not last. Delta has a code and has lasted. All of us and our organizations should have a code of ethics.

But how does one develop a code of ethics? It's really not that hard. It is simply stopping to think about our personal concept of what is right and wrong in a general sense, writing it down, and thinking about it when decisions are being made. Here are a few examples that can help us develop a better sense of character and a personal code of ethics:

- *Multiple religious teachings*: Treat others as we would like to be treated. Almost every religion in the world has this statement embedded in its core teachings. There is a reason for that. Thinking through how treating others applies to our own conduct as well as that of our business can be the foundation to developing a code. Other considerations include employees, customers, family members, peers, and even competitors.

- *The Rotary four-way test on what we think, say, or do*: (1) Is it the truth? (2) Is it fair to all concerned? (3) Will it build good will and better friendships? (4) Will it be beneficial to all concerned?[2]

- *The Kiwanis Objects, a few of which are*: (1) To give primacy to the human and spiritual rather than material values of life. (2) To encourage the living of the golden rule. (3) To promote higher social business, and professional standards.[3]

- *Seek the counsel of mentors*: Have discussions with people who have had experience and who have "been there and done that."

As we grow older, we have a duty to pass on what we have learned along the way. Others have a duty to tap that wisdom if they want to have a code of ethics. Developing mentors is a great way to gain experience without having to make all the same mistakes.

- *Read and think*: Simple efforts to determine who we want to be.

We all understand we should have a concept of right and wrong. Where the line is drawn is critical at sea as well in our jobs ashore and in our families at home. The *Costa Concordia* went down because of a failure of both accountability and ethics.

3. Have Only One Set of Ethics

Gen. David Petraeus was one of the most brilliant strategic thinkers the U.S. military had had in its long history. After a highly successful military career, he became the director of the Central Intelligence Agency. He was forced to resign that post when it became known that he had been involved in an extramarital affair with his biographer. He should no longer be considered by all to be a great leader.[4]

There are different views on his resignation. On the one hand are those who maintain that a person's private life does not impact their professional performance. Their opinion is that Petraeus' contributions to the nation were far more significant than his infidelity; thus there is no reason for him to resign. On the other hand, there are those who see no separation between professional and personal lives when it comes to ethics. Why should someone be trusted at work when they cannot be trusted at home? How can we expect soldiers and sailors to follow into harm's way someone who lies and cheats? If someone can treat his spouse with such disregard, what makes us think he will treat his soldiers and sailors any differently?

A captain is in the second group. There can be no separation between right and wrong in different environments. Conduct ashore is as important as conduct afloat. An officer who gets a drunk driving conviction ashore has probably ended his or her military career. A crew learns to trust a captain not only by what they see on ship but also what they see ashore.

We all establish a level of trust with our families, friends, business associates, customers, and others in the community we know and don't know. Achieving a high level of trust is dependent on what everyone else sees in our everyday life, not just what we do at the office. Conduct on the golf course, during Little League games, when borrowing tools from a neighbor, or paying off loans, and so on are small but important parts of building trust. The big one is that if we cannot be trusted at home with our families, how can we expect anyone to trust us in business?

Real Trust Is a Product to Sell

At a recent business retreat for a bank, I listened to several presentations on ways to create a good experience for customers: welcome on arrival, fast service, personal attention, etc. As the presenters admitted, their loan rates and savings rates were not significantly different from those of other banks. So they needed to differentiate themselves by the experience whenever customers visited the bank.

I gave them another reason in my presentation: trust. If all banks for the most part offer the same services, and if all banks are protected by the FDIC, what truly differentiates a bank is how much each bank employee can be trusted to provide honest service and advice to customers. If I know I can trust the business loan officer, I'll do business with him or her. But how do I know that?

The same is true of most every profession: doctors, lawyers, real estate agents, and construction companies—everyone, when we really think about it. We don't use a real estate company to lease office space; we use an agent we think we can trust. We are indifferent to the name of the agent's company. The agent has probably shifted companies a number of times. So how do we know whom to trust?

If we want ourselves and our companies to succeed in a business environment where other peers and products are similar, creating trust should be a top priority. How we play golf with rules that require personally imposed penalties, act in social gatherings, treat our family members, treat others, follow rules, etc., are all outside the office. They are also the key to selling ourselves as people who can be trusted. Selling trust starts outside the office. Once earned outside the office, it becomes a key business advantage for individuals and for companies.

We want to do business with people we trust. They earn our trust by knowing their job and conducting themselves in and out of the office in a way we trust. That way is established first by developing a code of ethics.

Questions for Discussion or Reflection

1. How do you personally determine what is right and wrong?
2. Who do you really trust? Why?
3. Can personal and business ethics be separated?
4. How do you create trust with your clients in your business?
5. How do you achieve job competence?

"Aye, Aye, Sir!"
Motivational Leadership

Japanese task force, on the horizon to the right, lands a salvo astern of the USS *Kitkun Bay* (CVE 71). Beyond the carrier, a smokescreen is being laid by destroyer escorts to cover the carrier in her escape. Off Leyte Gulf, October 25, 1944. (U.S. Naval Institute Photo Archive)

October 1944

On the morning of October 25, 1944, a group of escort aircraft carriers and a few destroyers were operating near the island of Luzon, assisting in Gen. Douglas MacArthur's amphibious assault on the Philippines at Leyte Gulf. Unknown to this small fleet was that the larger fleet of

Adm. Bull Halsey had been decoyed away from its protecting stations by an approaching Japanese carrier fleet, and a large Japanese task force of four battleships, eight cruisers, and eleven destroyers slipped behind Halsey and approached the escort carrier group. The first indication the American ships had of the enemy's presence was when their masts became visible fifteen miles away and large fourteen-inch shells began to fall amid the carriers.

At this point the battle off Samar Island commenced and has since been called the greatest military mismatch in history. Arrayed against the largest surface group the Japanese had gathered in World War II were four American destroyers whose largest weapons were five-inch guns. They faced fourteen-inch guns.

Adm. Clifton Sprague commanded the small American force. He had little choice when the attack began. "Small boys attack!" he commanded while the carriers turned away. The next two hours represented one of the defining qualities of the U.S. Navy: motivation to enthusiastically follow orders.

Outnumbered and outgunned, the U.S. destroyers headed directly for the Japanese battleships. As shells struck the destroyers, they made smoke and fired every weapon and their torpedoes. On one sinking destroyer, only one gun was still in action. A loader continued to yell down to the magazine crew, "More shells! More shells!"

Three American destroyers were sunk in the attack, but the confusion caused by the smoke, torpedoes, and gunfire influenced the Japanese admiral to withdraw his ships. He mistakenly believed the Americans had many more ships in action than just a few destroyers. The destroyer attack prevented the loss of thousands of lives afloat on the ships and troops ashore. My father was one of those troops ashore.

In his book *History of United States Naval Operations in World War II*, naval historian Samuel Morison described the action: "In no engagement of its entire history has the United States Navy shown more gallantry, guts and gumption than in those two morning hours between 0730 and 0930 off Samar."

What made the ship captains and crews so motivated that they all said "aye, aye, sir," turned immediately, and attacked with enthusiasm? It was more than just obeying an order. It was motivation developed long before the order.

"Aye, aye, sir" is the naval expression used by sailors that means more than just "yes." It means "yes" with enthusiasm and an implicit indication that an order will be carried out to the best of the sailor's ability. The simple response of "yes" to an order, somewhat like saying "okay," is not a naval tradition. Captains and crews never respond with just "yes, sir" to an order.

Creating Motivation

"Aye, aye, sir" reflects motivation. Motivated leaders and crews are critical to winning battles. The same can be said for competitive businesses ashore. How that motivation is developed afloat and ashore is very similar. There are three ways to create it.

Know the "Why" of Our Team

Late at night I often wandered the ship to see how things were going with the night watches. While I was frequently on the bridge or in the CIC, I was not as often in the engine rooms or smaller places, such as the supply department spaces.

As much as I wanted to know what was going on, I also wanted the sailors on watch to know I was interested and cared about what they were doing. These late-night wanderings were also a good time to check on morale and motivation. It was important to the safety of the ship and the accomplishment of our mission that the crew be enthusiastic about their jobs and mission.

What I learned during these late-night sessions has since been summarized in a TED talk by Ted Sinek that focused on why we do what we do.[1] As he points out, we all know what we are supposed to do and are always learning how to do it, but we need to also focus on why we do what we do. What motivates us? Knowing that makes us better leaders.

For my sailors, I not surprisingly found that their underlying motivation was their belief that they were protecting their country and their families. All sailors and officers take an oath of allegiance, which in part says "I will support and defend the Constitution of the United States against all enemies." That's a pretty serious job description. And we take that oath seriously. It's the main reason our military has the battle record it has.

But this first motivation prompted a second motivation that was just as important. My sailors were motivated to not let their shipmates down, to do their job, to be dependable. We all recognized that our lives at sea depended on each other. In order to succeed, we had to be a team. Motivation at sea has not changed since the lone gunner in 1944 yelled, "More shells!" as his ship was sinking.

In our companies ashore there is obviously no oath of office to defend the United States. There is also not as much motivation to take care of our coworkers such as sailors have to take care of their shipmates. No medals are awarded. With so many differences, what can leaders ashore learn from captains at sea? In fact, a lot.

Take bankers, for example. What motivates them to be in banking or to do a good job in whatever position they have? What is so motivating about making loans every day? Can they be motivated to do the same this year as last year?

The first answer, but by far not the last, is money. Bankers work for a paycheck. With their pay, they are able to live a particular lifestyle. If a banker does especially good work, a bonus might be involved. Money is always first on their mind. Right?

Maybe not. Money is just a tool to support what we are motivated to do. It is not the real motivation as to why bankers are bankers. If they really thought about it, bankers do what they do because of the satisfaction they have in not only helping themselves to productive lives but of helping others have productive lives too.

Bankers don't just make home loans; they help people have homes for their families. They don't just make business loans; they help businesses grow and create more jobs. In short, without bankers, we would not have the productive communities in which we live and work.

It's the same for other professions. Orthodontists don't just fix teeth; they make people feel better about themselves. Lawyers don't just solve disputes; they allow a community to live in a civilized manner. Sailors don't just fire weapons systems; they protect a way of life in America.

The first mission statement of Apple Computer was not to build the best computers, but "to make a contribution to the world by making tools for the mind that advances humankind." That mission statement appealed to a talented pool of computer experts. The results are history. Motivation comes from doing something that means something. Apple's employees were motivated for a mission in the same way as sailors are motivated.

So what do ship captains and leaders ashore have in common when motivating their crew or employees? They both need to concentrate on why they do what they do. With that, everyone can work with the spirit of "aye, aye, sir."

Create Pride through Training

Navy ships actually have advertising billboards on them. The crew can't see them because they are painted on the side of the ship. But to everyone else they are very visible. The advertising is not for a product but for showing the fleet how well this particular ship operates.

The signs are what the Navy calls battle excellence awards. Each warfare area on a ship can earn an E for excellence and have that letter painted on the side of the bridge. Good ships have many E's painted in different colors to indicate which warfare area has earned the award. The best ships have a large white E painted on the side. Sailors are rightly proud to be on a ship with a big white E.

Ships with pride seem to continually operate best. Pride breeds on itself. Although about a quarter of a ship's crew rotates off every year, new crew members quickly sense the existing pride and work hard to maintain it. When sailors are looking for their next assignment, ships with excellence awards are the ones most requested.

Creating pride is one of the best ways a captain can lead his or her crew. That's because the captain is the one person who can most influence the performance of the crew and the way the ship operates. Both performance and operations result from mainly one source: training. A well-trained ship equals a ship that earns battle excellence awards. Earning excellence awards creates pride. Thus training creates a confident crew.

As I related earlier, I learned the training lesson a few weeks into my first assignment as an ensign on a destroyer. I noticed a sailor apprentice was swabbing the deck but not cleaning the swab periodically. He was just spreading the dirt evenly on that part of the deck. When his chief petty officer saw what he was doing, he gave the sailor a tongue-lashing that I remember to this day: "How can you be so stupid," he yelled. The rest of what he said can't be printed.

I thought about that over the following weeks and realized that the sailor apprentice had not been trained to correctly swab a deck. It was really the chief's fault, not the sailor's fault. From swabbing the deck to firing missiles, training became a focus for the rest of my career. As a result, my crews won many white excellence awards. On the USS *Cape St. George*, they won the USS *Arizona* Memorial Award for being the most combat-ready surface ship in the entire Navy.

My most memorable moment on training came just before the first Gulf War, while a television reporter was interviewing a gunner's mate.

"Are you afraid?" asked the reporter.

"No, sir," the sailor answered. "We are so well trained that I am confident we can handle any emergency."

How does a captain's focus on creating pride through training translate to businesses and other organizations ashore? After all, they're not swabbing decks or firing missiles in a war zone. How do we instill pride in a company that distributes tires, a law firm, or a government agency?

While each organization is different, the training process that creates pride is the same: train people for their job and for their supervisor's job as well. Give them the training to better their chances for a successful career in the company. Train them even if it means they might go to another company with the extra expertise. If there are supervisory jobs, provide not only technical training for the position but human resource management training in skills like leadership.

The Atlanta Police Department recently established a leadership training institute for all levels of the organization, from police recruits to deputy chiefs. This institute teaches leadership and management. The chief of the Atlanta Police Department had recognized that his officers were getting the technical training they needed at each level, such as sergeant and lieutenant, but they weren't receiving any training in how to be a supervisor or a leader.

Now, at each level, officers must take a number of online or classroom courses to be considered for promotion. The results have been a higher retention of officers, better performance, and a drop in crime rates. Officers are now proud to be in the Atlanta Police Department. Training like this can be done in any organization.

The key to pride is to have a formal training program monitored by the captain or organization head. With training comes excellent performance. With excellent performance comes pride. And with pride comes an organization that will continue to excel year after year. It all starts with some attention from the top ranks of an organization.

Pride results in the motivating spirit of "aye, aye, sir."

Show You Really Care for Your Employees

Sleeping accommodations for sailors are not what many would consider comfortable and spacious. A berthing space may have around thirty sailors living in three-tier bunk beds with one head (bathroom). Each sailor has a small vertical locker for hanging uniforms and a rectangular box under the mattress for storing everything else. It's not much space. But then sailors wear the same thing every day, so variety is unnecessary.

I often wandered through the berthing areas during the day to check their cleanliness and generally chat with the crew members. When doing so I noticed that most crew members had pictures of their families or girlfriends taped inside their rectangular storage area. We would chat about whomever was in the pictures, especially their children.

I enjoyed getting to know each member of the crew. It was a fun part of the job of being captain. I also wanted them to know I cared about their families too. While I never said it, the pictures always reminded me that my job was to make sure all the sailors got back safely to their families ashore. I wanted them to be able to see their daughter's soccer games. The pictures always reminded me of my accountability for operations, safety, and the morale of the crew. I needed to make sure I was taking care of my crew.

Taking care of the crew or employees is a part of most every company mission statement. But what does that really mean?

A captain at sea has a much broader responsibility for caring for the crew than does his or her counterparts ashore. A captain is responsible for feeding, clothing, housing, training, instilling professionalism, and maintaining morale both, of the sailors and their families ashore. There are no equivalent roles in organizations ashore. But that does not mean caring for employees should be any less important. There are still a lot of lessons to learn.

When leaders ashore think of taking care of their employees, we generally think of compensation, bonuses, vacation time, safety, and treating employees fairly. Those are all necessary, but leaders can adapt some ship captain initiatives too. I believe there are three important goals to add to the preceding list: create a personable environment, have concern for families too, and help employees get better jobs at other companies if their current job has no room for promotion.

Create a Personable Working Environment

One of the traditions on most ships is that the captain invites the officers to his or her home to welcome new officers and say farewell to those departing. My wife, Sheila, and I did that for years, but it was only after a few years of doing it that I realized how important it was to have the officers and some crew members to my home and how important it was to visit their homes too.

When you visit another home, you get to know who lives there. You see pictures, meet family members, pet the dog, and generally get a feel for the family. We gain a family perspective that's only available in each home. That perspective carries over to the ship. I knew more about an officer and was better able to relate to him because I had visited his home, and he was able to understand me better because he had visited mine. It allowed me to create a personable environment on the ship. Topics of conversation on the bridge during a slow night were now much more interesting than talking about who was leading in the standings of a particular league.

Entertaining direct reports at home is not frequently done by organizational leaders ashore. That's too bad. It's one of the most important ways to motivate employees. If they get to know the boss better, they become more loyal and productive. Leaders can go a long way toward taking care of their employees when they create an understanding of an employee's life outside the office. It becomes a more personable environment at work.

Show Concern for Families

A ship sails over the horizon and is gone for months. My experience has been that as soon as we left port, a number of washing machines broke, several cars stopped working, many roofs started leaking, quite a few children got sore throats, many dogs ran off . . . the list goes on and on. The worst was that crew members promised to mail their paycheck home each month, forgetting that the mail sometimes took more than a month to get home.

All these crises are important to a ship captain, because if a family is not happy, a crew member will not be either. If a crew member is concerned for his or her family back home, that crew member's performance on board may not be as good as it can be. Thus captains are concerned about families too.

Recognizing this challenge to morale and performance has resulted in formal support programs by the Navy and the creation of a family ombudsman (the spouse of a crew member) for each ship. When problems arose like having no money because the check was in the mail, there were people and processes in place to help.

Businesses ashore may not need that level of support, but the idea of providing assistance to families should be a part of every leader's efforts to create a motivated workforce. Things like money-management classes, grief counseling, good communication on work benefits, care for families who survive the death of an employee, and holding fun events that include families are a few examples. A family newsletter from the ship was a big morale boost to the families ashore. Taking care of families is really just doing a lot of little things that add up over time.

Walking Around Again

We've looked at this several times already, but the topic cannot receive too much emphasis. A captain does a lot of walking. Since the captain is accountable for everything, getting a feel about how things are working around the ship can never be gained from sitting in the captain's chair on the bridge all day. I'd find all types of things of interest: the cakes being baked in the galley were all tilted forty-five degrees because a few hours ago I had turned the ship too sharply at just the wrong time (I promised to never do that again and ate a part of the small end of the cake); a repainted deck area looked terrific (I thanked the deck seamen); an oil leak was being fixed by engineers who were ruining their uniforms in the process (I made a note to replace the uniforms at the ship's expense). There was always something serious going on as well as something humorous.

But the most important thing about walking around is that I met the crew more often, and the sailors got a chance to talk with me. I could pick up from these conversations what was going well or not so well in their eyes.

I managed to visit certain pulse points more often than other parts of the ship. One of these was the forward paint storage room, which I mentioned earlier. The area was hard to access. I needed to climb down three sets of vertical ladders and open and close several watertight hatches along the way.

I went there because I had learned that if the remotest areas of the ship were well maintained, then almost every process on the ship functioned well. If a remote storage area was maintained, then the mind-set of doing things right probably applied to the weapons systems and every other part of the ship too. My walks around the ship revealed how motivated the crew was when they said, "aye, aye, sir."

"Aye, aye" may mean "yes," but it means "yes" with enthusiasm and motivation. Creating a motivated working environment is the job of every captain and leader ashore. Knowing why a crew works, creating pride through training, and creating a caring working environment are all ways a captain creates and maintains a motivated crew. Leaders ashore can use the same practices with their company's employees.

Questions for Discussion and Reflection

1. What is the real why behind your organization?
2. How can you motivate your employees by focusing on the why behind their actions?
3. Does every employee in your company have a training plan?
4. How do you personally show you care about your employees?

The Corner Office and the Captain's Chair

Captain's chair on USS *Midway* (CV 41). (Wikimedia Commons/Tenji)

June 1775

News of the battles of Lexington and Concord reached the coastal town of Machias, Maine, in May 1775. As the fever of rebellion rose over the following weeks, the townspeople erected a liberty pole in the center of the town in defiance of British control. When the British warship HMS *Margaretta* arrived in June and demanded that the liberty pole be taken down, the town refused. So the British captain threatened to fire on the town.

On June 12, 1775, what might be considered the first naval engagement of the Revolutionary War occurred, though independence had not yet been declared and a Continental navy did not yet exist. June 12 may also be the first date in American history when the commonality of leadership between business ashore and action at sea was demonstrated.

Under the cover of darkness, Jeremiah O'Brien, a local lumber businessman, led a band of farmers and businessmen in some small rowboats across the harbor. Sneaking onto another ship in the harbor with mostly axes and pitchforks for weapons, they captured it and then moved next to the *Margaretta*, which they attacked and captured. It was the first time a British ship had surrendered to Americans.

My first command, the destroyer USS *O'Brien*, was named in honor of Jeremiah O'Brien, the man who led that assault.

Who says there is little connection between business environments ashore and naval environments at sea? The two have very much in common.

Accountable leadership ("no excuse, sir") means more things go right and fewer things go wrong because of the pressure a leader feels when that leader considers himself or herself accountable for most everything. Motivated to keep the British ship from firing on their town, the businessmen of Machias did not let the fact they had no guns deter them from an innovative night attack with pitchforks.

Thinking-ahead leadership ("I'll find out, sir") results from the pressure of accountability. This pressure makes us train and retrain ourselves and our employees. The businessmen who captured HMS *Margaretta* did not attack without a plan and some practice. They trained on how to board a ship in the dark, and then they did it.

Ethics ("yes, sir/no, sir") were the foundation of their action: submitting to British rule was not acceptable. They knew when they were being treated right and when they were not.

Motivational leadership ("aye, aye, sir!") created the enthusiasm for a group of farmers and merchants to take on an armed British ship.

The Captain's Chair

The captain's chair on the bridge of a ship has traditionally been the only chair there. Everyone else is standing a watch for a few hours while the captain may need to spend a whole day and sometimes the whole night in the pilothouse. So the captain gets a chair.

It's also a symbol of the leader who is accountable to maneuver the ship safely in accomplishing an assigned mission. The chair is always on the starboard (right) side of the bridge because the nautical rules of the road require the captain to maneuver to avoid any other ship approaching from the right. The other ship has the right of way.

On top of that, the chair in the central control area of the ship is a symbol of the captain's responsibility to create the operational goals, set the objectives, monitor progress, and thus lead the organization. The chair is in many senses the captain's office. It's there where the captain receives reports, directs communications, holds meetings (everyone else stands, which makes for shorter meetings), and thinks.

The corner office. (Courtesy Kimball Office)

The Corner Office

Since many company leaders have the best office at the company headquarters, we can generally find them on the top floor and in the corner office with the best view. Sounds like the location of the captain's chair: top deck and horizon view. But the same can be said of many other offices in the company for department and division leaders, just not as high.

The corner office, like the captain's chair, is a symbol of a leader's status. When we walk into one, we know we are talking to someone with authority and responsibility. Decisions that affect the company are made there. The big picture of operations comes together there.

When the occupant walks into a corner office, he or she is reminded of the accountability they have to make the right decisions and pull together the big picture. Like the captain's chair, it is the center of the company for goal setting, planning, and execution.

The Corner Office and the Captain's Chair

When we look out the windows of the corner office or the captain's chair, and after we get over how far they are able to see, we realize there is not that much difference between the leadership role of a ship captain and the leadership role of a business or organization leader. At first glance that may be hard to grasp, because one window may be covered with salt spray and the other is floor to ceiling, but leading people is basically the same from both locations.

It's the same even though the chair or office occupants operate in different environments. The structure of the military environment is different from that of a business, but leading people in the military is not. Gone are the days of hanging sailors from the yardarm for rule infractions. Gone are the days where motivation through intimidation made up for a lack of good leadership. Captain Bligh would lose his crew in a few minutes if he tried his torturous discipline tactics today. Those days faded quickly a long time ago and disappeared completely with a volunteer military.

Today's military environment is much the same as that of any business or organization. Sailors must be led, not just ordered around. Sailors must be motivated, not just ordered around. A captain who tries to lead by just giving orders will not be a very good—or successful—captain. The only noticeable difference between the two cultures is that motivation in the military is easier than in civilian businesses. But there is a lesson there too.

"I swear that I will support and defend the Constitution of the United States" is an oath taken by every sailor, officer and enlisted, when they join the Navy. Big mission. Big motivator.

"A Global Force for Good" is a recent motto for the Navy.

"Don't give up the ship!" and "I have not yet begun to fight!" have been battle cries since the beginning of the U.S. Navy.

Sailors join the Navy because of this meaningful calling to make the world a better place and to protect the American way of life in the process. They take the oath seriously. It's a potentially life-or-death decision to join, so the motivation of a higher cause is necessary for someone to volunteer.

Employees, of course, don't take an oath to defend their country. That is not the mission of businesses. There is no one outside of the military who is willing to give their life to make sure their company does not go bankrupt.

I'm frequently asked why more merchant seaman don't shoot back when they are being boarded by pirates. The answer is motivation. If no hostage has lost his or her life after being captured, why would a civilian sailor give his or her life for a shipping company? Better to be a captive than be dead. The opposite is true for a Navy sailor.

That company employees do not take an oath when they are hired, however, does not mean a business cannot motivate them like the Navy.

Take, for example, Apple when it was first formed. Its mission statement was "to make a contribution to the world by making tools for the mind that advances humankind." Note that it was not to "make the best computer in the world." Steve Jobs' approach of appealing to employees by offering jobs that "advance humankind" worked in gathering the most gifted computer geniuses in the industry. It was a motivation to a noble cause that, in part, has led to the success of Apple.

Any company can motivate its employees like Apple and the Navy. "Support and defend the Constitution" and a "contribution . . . that advances humankind" are not that much different.

Orthodontists do not just straighten teeth; they make people feel better and more confident about themselves. Bankers don't just lend money for mortgages; they help create a community so families can enjoy their lives together. Every profession has a higher calling beyond just swabbing decks.

The CEO Corner Office

When viewed from the window of a captain's chair, the leadership styles of business leaders have much in common with the leadership style of a ship captain. I have found it interesting since I retired from the Navy and spent sixteen years in business how often business leaders, when asked about their leadership styles, will respond with some point that follows the four leadership principles of a ship captain: personal accountability, thinking, ethics, and motivation.

The CEO or any leader's chair is not that much different from the captain's chair. Here are a few representative samples of comments by senior executives:

Accountability: "No Excuse, Sir!"

Brad Smith (CEO, Intuit, a software company)

Question: What about leadership lessons early in your career?

Answer: I spent six years in a job prior to Intuit, doing a range of jobs in marketing. I started the Internet division . . . convinced the board to give us $40 million . . . telling them we could sell more things online than our sales force could sell. I told them we wouldn't even need a sales force. After $40 million, we sold just fifteen units.

So when I went to meet with the board, I figured I was going to get fired. I called my parents, and my dad said, "Just go in and say: 'Here is what I thought. Here's what happened. Here's where I was wrong, and here's what I would do differently.'"

I did that, and when I was finished, one board member started clapping and said, "You are more valuable to us now . . . for three reasons . . . you won't make that mistake again . . . your engineers built a killer product, and our salespeople now have something they can put in their sales bag . . . the street thinks we are old school and they're going to do everything online. You just proved that is not likely, so we're smarter as a result.

That taught us to fail forward.[1]

Robert Balentine (chairman and CEO, Balentine, a wealth management company)

Question: When you created Balentine, what was your goal in establishing a company culture?

Answer: No silos. I wanted a company with a culture that is focused on the overall success of the company, not just the individual. It's important that leaders set that tone at the top; I make that point at every weekly staff meeting. To back that philosophy up, everyone's incentive compensation is based on the success of the company. If someone brings in a new relationship, they are not individually rewarded with a larger bonus.

They understand their success is dependent on the success of the company. Everyone feels accountable for the success of the company.

We hire people who can fit into our culture by looking closely at their character in addition to their investment acumen. You can tell a lot about a person by taking time to talk with them outside the office—at dinner, for example. How does a potential employee interact with their spouse or the wait staff? We also look at how a potential employee gives back to his or her community. What is it they do for others? That tells a lot about their character.[2]

Pete Correll (chairman and CEO, Georgia Pacific, a manufacturing company)

Question: What is one aspect of your leadership style?

Answer: Good news flies up the flagpole. Bad news flounders at every level of an organization. Bad news does not get better with time. I'd tell my team to tell me what they don't want to tell me because they think they can solve it before I find out. I want to know the bad news.

I've found it's hard to change the culture of a company. It's easier to change the people than to change the culture. When employees discover that approach, they change and the culture changes.[3]

Thinking Ahead and Learning: "I'll Find Out, Sir!"

Michael Polk (Newell Rubbermaid, a manufacturing company)

Question: What leadership lessons did you learn early in your career?

Answer: When I graduated from college I thought I knew everything I needed to know to run a manufacturing plant. I learned the first day that I did not know anything. I had to learn how to really get things done from the line operators who had being doing the basics for years to managers with more experience than me. I had to accept that I did not know it all.[4]

Adm. James Stavridis, USN (Ret.) (former supreme allied commander of NATO and currently the dean of the Fletcher School of Law and Diplomacy at Tufts University).

On his list of "Tricks of the Trade: How Leaders Make Things Happen":

> Carve out time to think. Too many leaders spend so much of their
> time putting out brush fires that they lose sight of the fact that they

may be in the wrong forest. . . . It's crucial that a leader demand of his team that they provide enough time for thinking. There is always a tendency to fill the white space—don't let your schedulers do that.[5]

Ethics: "Yes, Sir! No, Sir!"

Frank Skinner (former president and CEO, BellSouth Telecommunications)

Question: What was a key trait you looked for when interviewing a potential employee?

Answer: When I conducted an interview, my first goal was to determine if this person had integrity. A person with integrity will always do the right thing and is also a person who has respect for others: fellow employees, customers, stockholders, anyone with whom they come into contact. Respect for others is a key to a successful company.[6]

Paul Garcia (CEO, Global Payments, a financial services firm)

Question: How do you develop a corporate culture of change?

Answer: Our strategic plan has a vision for the near term and the long term in quantifiable terms, but we also emphasize that we should do the right thing. The Rotary Four Way Test of the things we think or do is a good basis for creating a culture of doing the right thing: Is it the truth? Is it fair to all concerned? Will it build good will and better friendships? Will it be beneficial to all concerned?[7]

Motivation: "Aye, Aye, Sir!"

Steve Hennessy (co-owner of Hennessy Automobiles, Atlanta, GA)

Question: How do you motivate employees in the highly competitive automotive sales business?

Answer: By simply saying thank you to employees when they do a good job; by providing a working environment where employees can have an appropriate free rein and can have all the support and training they need; and by creating a balanced life-work environment that recognizes the need for employees to have time with their families.[8]

Adm. William H. McRaven, USN (Ret.) (former commander of the United States Special Operations Command and currently chancellor of the University of Texas System)

The first of his ten lessons from SEAL training that can help people change the world:

"If you make your bed every morning you will have accomplished the first task of the day. It will give you a small sense of pride and it will encourage you to do another task and another and another. By the end of the day, that one task completed will have turned into many tasks completed. Making your bed will also reinforce the fact that little things in life matter. If you can't do the little things right, you will never do the big things right.

"And, if by chance you have a miserable day, you will come home to a bed that is made—that you made—and a made bed gives you encouragement that tomorrow will be better.

"If you want to change the world, start off by making your bed."[9]

Leaders who sit in the captain's chair or the corner office have power. How they handle that power is much the same.

The October 2015 issue of *Atlanta* magazine listed its pick of the top fifty-five most powerful people in the Atlanta metropolitan area and asked them their reflections on how to acquire power and how to use it. Here are a few of the responses:[10]

David Cummings (CEO of Atlanta Ventures): "Culture is the only sustainable competitive advantage that's completely within the control of the entrepreneur."

Mark Becker (president of Georgia State University): "Never lose focus and never lie. That way your decision making will be uncluttered, your motives transparent, and your integrity intact."

Kevin Riley (editor of the *Atlanta Journal-Constitution*): "You can't understand the world from afar, or from a twitter feed. Seek information. Go experience it. Talk to people. Go deep and learn their stories."

Doug Hertz (president and CEO of United Distributors, Inc.): "There is a difference between power and influence. If you are irresponsible with power, you'll lose your influence, and ultimately your ability to lead."

Good advice for leaders at sea and ashore.

Five Key Characteristics to Hiring or Being Hired

Bill Bartman's article "5 Characteristics to Look for in Every Potential New Hire" appeared in the April 13, 2010, *Business Insider*. In my experience of sitting in chairs on the ship's bridge and in a corner office, I found this article to be the single best summary of the key traits needed to be hired, eventually move into a corner office, and be effective once there.

His five characteristics are not surprising but good to remember: (1) aptitude, (2) attitude, (3) intelligence, (4) intensity, and (5) integrity. The four key leadership traits of sea captains—no excuse, sir; I'll find out, sir; yes/no, sir; and aye, aye, sir—cover all of these areas, so learning the four is good for covering his five. For some, the four may be easier than the five. Below is a summary of the five.

Aptitude: Can this potential employee perform the job? Is he or she qualified to fire missiles? Aptitude requires a demonstrated sense of personal and business accountability, an ability to learn and think ahead, a sense of ethics, and enthusiasm. All four leadership traits of sea captains combine to create an attitude that creates aptitude.

Attitude: Can this potential employee perform the job with a positive spirit, a desire to learn, and an ability to work as a team member? Does he or she want to qualify as a tactical action officer who is trusted to fire missiles? An attitude of personal accountability creates a professional attitude across all areas, especially in the leadership of employees. It starts with a "no excuse, sir!" attitude of accountability.

Intelligence: Can this potential employee think ahead and always try to learn? This has nothing to do with IQ. Does he or she want to be captain or work from the corner office and is he or she able to think creatively and be motivated by an internal desire to always be learning and thus looking for new ways of doing business? It starts with an attitude of "I'll find out, sir!"

Intensity: Can this potential employee work with enthusiasm? Does he or she have the internal drive and work ethic to someday sit in the captain's chair or corner office? It starts with the "aye, aye, sir!" attitude for motivation.

Integrity: Can this potential employee be trusted? Does he or she have a sense of what is right and wrong? Can customers trust this person to do what he or she has promised to do? Will employees see this person's integrity at the office and at home? It starts with answering a question truthfully with a "yes, sir" or "no, sir" attitude of firm ethics.

Three Thousand Years

"I have not yet begun to fight!" answered Capt. John Paul Jones when asked by a British ship captain to surrender.

"Don't give up the ship!" yelled Capt. James Lawrence at the battle of Lake Erie after being mortally wounded.

"Damn the torpedoes! Full speed ahead!" ordered Adm. David Farragut in Mobile Bay as the lead ship in his column struck a mine and blew up.

These orders were not spur-of-the-moment decisions. They were not surprise decisions. They were not just reactive decisions. They were, as Steven Covey might call them, proactive decisions. Being "proactive" is the first habit in Covey's book, *7 Habits of Highly Effective People.*

The battle orders were decisions that, in fact, had been made long before they needed to be made. Those who gave the orders were ready to make them even though they did not know in advance they would have to make them. They were ready because they had learned the four traits of successful sea captains early in their careers, had practiced them for years, and were thus ready to utilize them when the critical time arrived.

They had inherited the four leadership traits of ship captains built over thousands of years of people going to sea. It probably all started when the first ship set sail without someone in charge and didn't come back. Over the following centuries of crews surviving storms and battles at sea, the leadership traits of ship captains were molded such that decisions like those of Jones, Lawrence, and Farragut were almost automatic. Accountability, learning and thinking, ethics, and enthusiasm all combined to make the captains ready to respond.

Business managers can train themselves to be ready in the same way. The four leadership traits of ship captains can be the four leadership traits of business leaders. They are not new leadership traits but are traits that allow leaders to look at leadership from a different perspective.

June 1996: Departing

"I stand relieved," I said at the change-of-command ceremony. Two years earlier I had said, "I relieve you, sir" as I took command. Now I turned it over to the next commanding officer.

When I departed the ship for the last time, the officer of the deck announced, "Captain, United States Navy, departing." For two years the announcement had been, "*Cape St. George*, departing." Now another officer had taken my place. He was now *Cape St. George*, and he now had the personal accountability of command that I had had for two years.

As I look back at my careers in the Navy and at Turner Broadcasting, I find it easy to see how the first minute at the U.S. Naval Academy shaped my career and my life. I recognize now that the first minute didn't just happen. It was the result of centuries of experiences at sea woven into four leadership principles needed for survival. Thousands of ship captains had learned that to survive there can be only four responses:

"No excuse, sir!"

"I'll find out, sir!"

"Yes, sir/No, sir!"

"Aye, aye, sir!"

These four leadership traits are the basics for preventing organizational chaos described by the *Wall Street Journal* editorial on leadership at sea and ashore quoted early in this book: "When men lose confidence and trust in those who lead, order disintegrates into chaos and purposeful ships into floating derelicts."

In the end, learning and using the four leadership traits of sea captains creates trust and confidence in those who lead afloat or ashore. And trust and confidence go a long way toward success.

ACKNOWLEDGMENTS

There is a unique naval term called "shipmate." It's a term really only understood by those who serve together on a ship at sea. A shipmate is a person who has shared the challenges and trials of survival at sea. Over my decades on numerous ships, I have had the honor and privilege to serve with more than a thousand shipmates. To them I am grateful for their service and support. It has been an honor to be their shipmate.

The term "classmate" at the United States Naval Academy is also unique. We start our experiences together on day one of plebe summer boot camp and learn together over the next four years how to become naval officers. My fourth company classmates became my band of brothers and still are today.

I will always be indebted to Master Chief Boiler Technician Doug Davis. He was a master not only in running boilers for a steam-driven ship, but he was also a master at training young officers like me how to apply the Navy's leadership principles in real life.

I had the privilege of working for one of the finest commanding officers in the history of the Navy. When I was the executive officer on board the guided missile cruiser USS *Valley Forge* (CG 50), Capt. Ted Lockhart taught me how to apply the Navy's leadership principles to command at sea. He did so with grace, humor, professionalism, and a personal touch. When I was confronted a few years later with an unusual challenge as captain, I would often try to imagine how Ted Lockhart would solve it.

I am also grateful to those at Turner Broadcasting, who gave a ship captain an opportunity to work in one of the most professional, and most interesting, companies in the world. Ted Turner, former captain of the America's Cup winner *Courageous*, who also served in the Coast Guard, created and led one of the most innovative companies in the world. He told me "don't let us leak."

Tom Johnson, then chairman of CNN, showed me how ethical standards can exist in the news media. He was a great mentor for me in transitioning to the civilian world. Terry McGuirk, Wayne Pace, John Kampfe, and Phil Kent all provided support and, gratefully, funding for whatever initiatives I tried to do. To all of them I'm grateful for their advice and example of how best to lead a company.

I learned through working with the hundreds of employees in my Turner Properties division how to translate the Navy's leadership principles to business. I am grateful for their patience and understanding over the years.

I also learned the translation of Navy leadership principles to business from my fellow five hundred members at the Rotary Club of Atlanta. The club represents the finest of business leaders who show the connection between the Navy's leadership principles and those of business by following the Rotary Four Way Test on decisions: Is it the truth? Is it fair to all concerned? Will it build good will and better friendships? Will it be beneficial to all concerned?

The Naval Institute Press plays a vital role in keeping and teaching the great traditions of the United States Navy. I am grateful to my editor, Gary Thompson, who was most patient and professional in leading me through the production wickets of my first book.

Most importantly, however, I am grateful for the love and support of my wife Sheila. For the four decades we have been sailing life together she has been a great example of how to lead a family with love, patience, kindness, inspiration, and encouragement. Never a day went by at sea without my missing her. She has been a great mother to our son Powell, who has made both of us proud. They are the center of my life.

I have had jobs I liked and a family I loved. Life doesn't get any better than that.

NOTES

Chapter 3. "No Excuse, Sir!"

1. Diana Preston, *Lusitania, An Epic Tragedy* (New York: Bloomsburry USA, 2002), 229.

2. Eric Larson, *Dead Wake: The Last Crossing of the Lusitania* (New York: Crown Publishers, 2015), 348.

3. Editorial, *Wall Street Journal*, May 14, 1952.

4. Nick Bunkley, "Criminal Charges Still Possible for Some GM Employees, U.S. Says," *Automotive News,* Sept. 17, 2015, http://www.autonews.com/article/20150917/OEM11/150919816/criminal-charges-still-possible-for-some-gm-employees-u.s.-says.

5. Leon Stafford, "After Dramatic Day, Ex-CEO Gets 28 Years," *Atlanta Journal-Constitution,* Sept. 22, 2015.

6. "Costa Concordia: What Happened," BBC News, Feb. 10, 2015, http://www.bbc.com/news/world-europe-16563562.

Chapter 5. "Yes/No, Sir!"

1. "Costa Concordia: What Happened," BBC News, Feb. 10, 2015, http://www.bbc.com/news/world-europe-16563562.

2. Rotary International, "Guiding Principles," https://www.rotary.org/myrotary/en/learning-reference/about-rotary/guiding-principles

3. Kiwanis International, "Guiding Objects," http://www.kiwanis.org/kiwanis/about-kiwanis/ourvalues#.VqOmKCorKUk

4. Greg Miller and Sari Hornitz, "David Petraeus Resigns as CIA Director," *Washington Post*, Nov. 9, 2012, https://www.washingtonpost.com/world/national-security/david-petraeus-resigns-as-cia-director/2012/11/09/636d204e-2aa8-11e2-bab2-eda299503684_story.html.

Chapter 6. "Aye, Aye, Sir!"

1. Simon Sinek, "How Great Leaders Inspire Action," TED Talk, August 14, 2014, https://www.ted.com/speakers/simon_sinek.

Conclusion

1. Adam Bryant, Corner Office, *New York Times*, April 12, 2014, http://www.nytimes.com/2014/04/13/business/brad-smith-of-intuit-follow-the-fastest-beat-of-your-heart.html?ref=business.

2. Robert Balentine, in discussion with the author, September 9, 2015.

3. Pete Correll, speech to Capital City Club Forum, Capital City Club, Atlanta, GA, September 21, 2015.

4. Michael Polk, speech to Rotary Club of Atlanta, Loudermilk Center, Atlanta, GA, September 14, 2015.

5. Adm. James G. Stavridis, USN (Ret.), *The Accidental Admiral: A Sailor Takes Command at NATO* (Annapolis, MD: Naval Institute Press, 2014), 132.

6. Frank Skinner, in discussion with the author, September 14, 2015.

7. Paul Garcia, speech to Rotary Club of Atlanta, Loudermilk Center, Atlanta, GA, September 22, 2015.

8. Steve Hennessy, in discussion with the author, September 15, 2015.

9. "Adm. McRaven Urges Graduates to Find Courage to Change the World," University of Texas at Austin news release, May 16, 2014, http://news.utexas.edu/2014/05/16/admiral-mcraven-commencement-speech.

10. "Lessons in Power," *Atlanta*, October 2015, 80.

ABOUT THE AUTHOR

Capt. Alec Fraser is a graduate of the U.S. Naval Academy. He has had two unique careers: he commanded two Navy missile ships and was later the president of a division of Turner Broadcasting. He was also an on-air military analyst for CNN and was a guest on the Larry King Show. While he was in command of the USS *Cape St. George* (CG 71), the ship earned the USS *Arizona* Memorial Trophy for being the most combat ready ship in the fleet.

The **Naval Institute Press** is the book-publishing arm of the U.S. Naval Institute, a private, nonprofit, membership society for sea service professionals and others who share an interest in naval and maritime affairs. Established in 1873 at the U.S. Naval Academy in Annapolis, Maryland, where its offices remain today, the Naval Institute has members worldwide.

Members of the Naval Institute support the education programs of the society and receive the influential monthly magazine *Proceedings* or the colorful bimonthly magazine *Naval History* and discounts on fine nautical prints and on ship and aircraft photos. They also have access to the transcripts of the Institute's Oral History Program and get discounted admission to any of the Institute-sponsored seminars offered around the country.

The Naval Institute's book-publishing program, begun in 1898 with basic guides to naval practices, has broadened its scope to include books of more general interest. Now the Naval Institute Press publishes about seventy titles each year, ranging from how-to books on boating and navigation to battle histories, biographies, ship and aircraft guides, and novels. Institute members receive significant discounts on the Press's more than eight hundred books in print

Full-time students are eligible for special half-price membership rates. Life memberships are also available.

For a free catalog describing Naval Institute Press books currently available, and for further information about joining the U.S. Naval Institute, please write to:

Member Services
U.S. Naval Institute
291 Wood Road
Annapolis, MD 21402-5034
Telephone: (800) 233-8764
Fax: (410) 571-1703
Web address: www.usni.org